DATE DUE   F.

Marketing Decisions for
European Operations in the U.S.

Research for Business Decisions, No. 4

Other Titles in This Series

Marketing Decisions
for European Operations
in the U.S.

by
Jacques L. Picard

umi
RESEARCH PRESS

Library of Congress Cataloging in Publication Data

Picard, Jacques L   1950-
   Marketing decisions for European operations in
the U. S.

   (Research for business decisions ; no. 4)
   Bibliography: p.
   Includes index.
   1. Marketing—United States—Decision-making.
2. Corporations, European—United States. 3. Subsidiary
corporations—United States. I. Title. II. Series.

HF5415.1.P48   658.8   78-24322
ISBN 0-8357-0956-6
ISBN 0-8357-0957-4 pbk.

To Marianne and Bernard Picard

CONTENTS

CHAPTER 1

SCOPE OF THE STUDY

I. Background of the Study

A. Location of Authority in Multinationals

Several studies have shown that the location of authority has important implications for marketing decision-making in multinational corporations. Indeed, it has been suggested that 1) standardization and coordination of marketing decision; 2) rationalization of product design, advertising and promotion and 3) strategic planning are all affected by the location of the decision-making authority.

If it might be advocated that dissimilarities between different markets are so important that centralization of marketing decision-making at headquarters would be detrimental to the subsidiaries' performances, some authors disagree. Keegan for example (2) contends that functions are all better fulfilled by an interactive or more centralized approach. Because of headquarters' responsibility in strategic planning, they should also be directly involved in the other market-decision functions at local levels. Strategic planning will be more effective if the home-office can intervene at local levels monitor market research; to standardize certain market measures (permitting the international comparison of marketing performances) and to eliminate the duplication of efforts. The use of an interactive marketing program responsive both to market differences and similarities could lead to "major international operating synergies."(2).

The question of the nature and degree of control over marketing decision to be accorded to the subsidiary or left to headquarters is still a subject of controversy, as is the related issue concerning the use of marketing standardization in multinationals[a] (although attempts have recently been made to delineate criteria for evaluating the product potential for advertising standardization (5)). These are, of course, two quite separate issues and must be carefully distinguished. *Marketing standardization* refers to the degree of similarity in the marketing activities, programs or policies of a multinational enterprise from one country to another, whereas in this study, *marketing control* is used to mean the degree of regulating influence exercised by the home-office over the activities of a subsidiary. In this context, autonomy is defined as the power or right of self-management.

Although standardization of marketing programs can be enforced by hierarchical authority and used as a control device, this is not necessarily the case. For example: executive officers of a subsidiary may decide that the advertising messages used by the parent company in the home country are suitable to their markets and adopt them with little or no modifications. In that instance, we have standardization of a specific marketing activity without interference from the home-office. On the other hand, control does not necessarily imply standardization; one could conceive of a situation in which headquarters imposed an advertising program especially designed for the market of a particular subsidiary. In that latter case, high degree of control would have been exercised without standardization of the specific program. Control and standardization are not equivalent.

The recurring debate over the feasibility and appropriateness of centralization of marketing decision-making in multinational operations has resulted in efforts to isolate the factors which influence the degree of autonomy enjoyed by the subsidiaries of multinational companies. A number of studies have been done and several exploratory variables found.[b]

However these studies have usually been concerned with U.S. - based multinationals and not with European-based firms.

B. American Subsidiaries of European Parents

1)   Rocour's findings.

The first major exception to this trend in research is Rocour's exploratory study which focuses on the American subsidiaries of European firms (6). He gathered his data c. 1962. His main finding was that U.S. manufacturing subsidiaries of European-based companies enjoyed so extremely high a degree of independence that many were almost or completely out of the line structure of the parent organization. This lack of control seemed to produce two separate companies rather than two associate members of one company. "The control exercised by the parent company was remote, often negative, and limited to a loose stockholder type of supervision (7)." The main reasons given for this laissez-faire attitude of parent companies toward their American subsidiaries were (7):

1)   The generally large size of the U.S. subsidiary relative to the size of the parent company which creates a favourable basis for autonomy.
2)   U.S. legal restrictions: The U.S. anti-trust laws calling for competition between parent company and subsidiary

motivates an independent set-up. Also the Buy American Act and the U.S. Security regulations forbidding the awarding of defense contracts to companies having kept direct ties with their foreign parent company call for independent management of the subsidiary.

3) The fact that most of the European companies surveyed by Rocour had not immediately entered the manufacturing stage in the U.S. but had started their operations with a sales agent or an import bureau, moving progressively to an assembly plant and thereafter to the production stage.[c]

4) The sophistication of the American market: Rocour refers to "certain technical and economic characteristics of the United States: *a stable market, with the highest income per capita in the world,* a large number of technicians, highly-developed research abundantly financed, the large size of the average company, and *fairly constant political, monetary and fiscal policies.*" The implication here is that, being in a much more sophisticated environment, the subsidiaries have to conduct their operations independently from the home-office located in "under-developed" Europe. Rocour also explains that since most American subsidiaries successfully managed their operations during the Second World War without any communication from the home-office, they have never come to need its recommendations. The parent company in Europe is not in much of a position to react by replacing his subsidiary managers. Two explanations might be found for this. Firstly, European headquarters have not rotated their managers among subsidiaries and the home-office. This policy is backfiring now and it provides a greater leverage to those who are in the United States. Secondly, there is a chronic shortage of managers in Europe mostly as a result of manpower losses during World War II. Thus when a manager becomes practically irreplaceable, he finds himself in a strong bargaining position. (7)"

We should keep in mind that these conclusions and explanatory hypotheses relate to the situation as it existed in 1962, at a time when the effects of the Second World War were much stronger than is true today. Indeed, the business environment has changed since 1962 and we might suspect that a number of the reasons given in Rocour's article have lost most of their relevance.

The manager shortage in Europe due to World War II losses has without any doubt been largely corrected in the thirty years since the end of the war. In fact, it should not have any effect on the generation of managers under 50 years of age. We could also assume that most of the people who managed the American subsidiaries of European companies in the early 1940's (and developed "independence habits" during the war) are no longer in position. A man who would have been 35 years old (age considered as minimal for senior management) in 1940 (time of cessation of normal communication between Europe and America) would be 70 years old in 1975 and therefore past the normal retirement age.

Secondly, with regard to sophistication of the U.S. versus the European market, the changes since 1962 have been very important. First, the gap in the gross national product and standard of living between the United States and most Western European countries has been drastically reduced since 1962 (See Appendix A), and most inhabitants of Western Europe (except Portugal, Spain and Southern Italy) enjoy a standard of living relatively close to the American. Consequently, Europe should now not be very far from the United States in terms of market sophistication. Moreover, the gap in net income between European and American upper and middle managers has not only diminished, but in some countries the widge is now in favor of Europeans. The president of the U.S. subsidiary of a French company reveals: "I needed badly a specific man working at the parent company in France. I wanted to hire him to come and work in the U.S.; the guy was getting a salary of 25,000 dollars a year in France, I offered him 35,000 dollars but he told me that he was not going to take the job for less than 45,000 dollars. I was amazed, but after he explained to me that he took into account the loss of the French governmental family allocations (he had a wife and four children), the higher income taxes in the U.S., the smaller number of vacation weeks...I had to agree with him, I could not hire him because it would have broken the salary scale of my organization here, but I must say that while 15 years or even 10 years ago home-office executives were trying to come here to get higher income, the situation today is different." Similar comments were often heard in French, German and Swiss companies.

In the fifties and early sixties, Europe still recovering from the war, parent company executives were very often earning a half or even a third the incomes of their homologues in the company's U.S. subsidiary. This phenomenon has certainly influenced the attitude of headquarters executives toward their U.S. affiliates (some people have trouble giving orders to better-paid colleagues). In any case, this state of affairs was a serious obstacle to the transfer of executives from one side of the Atlantic to the other. It was difficult to send a man to the U.S. from the parent company without giving him an American salary. Then, once he got higher pay, it was almost impossible to reduce this salary to European dimensions once the man was back home. That may have been one of the reasons why European headquarters had not rotated their managers between the United States and the home country at the time of Rocour's study. With regard to the remarks of Rocour on the United States as a stable market (with highly-developed and abundantly financed research, and fairly constant political, monetary and fiscal policies) they are certainly no more relevant to the United States in 1975 than they are for many Western European countries.

In general, it would seem that during the Post-World-War II period, many Europeans have developed an "inferiority complex" vis-a-vis the United States which did not encourage control by European parent companies over the activities of their U.S. subsidiaries. This "complex" which was certainly still in existence in 1962 should have disappeared or at least been reduced today for the reasons cited.

According to most witnesses, Europe has been tremendously Americanized during the last 10-15 years in terms of life-style (more and more private cars, refrigerators, T.V. sets, washing machines, supermarkets...) and management style: Many Europeans have received management training in the United States or in American-based European companies. This trend to similarity on both sides of the Atlantic might be expected to have a positive impact on control of the marketing activities of U.S. subsidiaries by European headquarters. Similarity carries a potential for standardization of marketing programs and standardization is very often monitored by headquarters.

Another important change since Rocour's research has been the wider use of the the newest developments in communication media between Europe and America. It became relatively cheaper to travel from one side of the Atlantic Ocean to the other and the introduction of jet planes on commercial flights (starting around the year 1960) made the travel faster. However, it was not until the mid-sixties that a flight to the United States ceased to be an event for the European businessman and came to be considered a normal part of business operations.

The transatlantic telephone did not operate well (i.e. speed and clarity of connection) until the late fifties and early sixties. Finally, telex has only come into general use in day-to-day communication during the last decade.

The larger use of these communication media, reducing the distance between European home-offices and American subsidiaries might be expected greatly to improve the frequency and quality of international communications and encourage control over subsidiary activities by headquarters.

Finally, important changes have taken place since 1962 with respect to the size of European direct investment in the U.S. and the number of manufacturing companies in the U.S. with European parents. In 1962 the U.S. Department of Commerce reported (8) a universe of 235 manufacturing subsidiaries of foreign companies in the U.S., 158 being European. (That publication defined a foreign subsidiary as: "A United States Corporation in which 25 percent or more or the voting stock was owned directly or indirectly by a foreign parent organization.") Rocour (9) reports a universe of 101 manufacturing subsidiaries with 50% or more European ownership.

In March 1974 the U.S. Department of Commerce (10) listed 1029 U.S. manufacturing and petroleum subsidiaries as affiliates of foreign companies - 754 were European. If we deduct the 43 companies where the European parent had only a minority interest and the petroleum companies, we get a total number of 711 U.S. manufacturing subsidiaries of European-based companies.

J. Arpan and D. Ricks (12) reported a "minimum" number of 1246 manufacturing, mining and petroleum companies in the U.S. that are directly or indirectly owned by a foreign company, a much higher number than that reported by the Department of Commerce. This number is considered by the authors as a minimum and they conclude (11): "In any case, though the exact dimension of foreign investment in the U.S. may not be perfectly known, one fact remains clear, the findings of our research show that the importance of foreign investment in the U.S. is not only growing, but is also of more importance than was assumed, and so too is the importance of further research on it." Among those 1246 companies listed, 966 would be European manufacturing subsidiaries.

However, we can assess that the Arpan and Ricks list is very far from being accurate (although we do not know to what extent the number reported by Rocour was correct). Their directory is supposed to give the names and addresses of subsidiaries with manufacturing operations in the U.S., but in fact it includes many sales agencies[d] (i.e., no manufacturing operations in the U.S.) and companies unknown at the address given. Therefore an approximation of the number of foreign and European manufacturing susidiaries in the U.S. is still a speculation. Yet, on the basis of the figure given by the Department of Commerce publication (10) the number of U.S. manufacturing subsidiaries with 50% or more European owership is certainly not less than 707 and consequently at least seven times the number given by Rocour.

With regard to the size of the European direct investment in the U.S. the actual estimate of total book value of European direct investment at year-end 1973 (the latest figure available) was 12,158 million dollars, 5,743 million dollars being in manufacturing investment (13). The estimate for year-end 1962 was 5,247 million dollars, 1,515 million being in manufacturing investment (14). In other words these figures show that the direct manufacturing investments of European companies in the U.S. have increased 379% from 1962 to 1973.

These changes in the number and size of European-based manufacturing subsidiaries in the U.S. are likely to have totally changed the overall pattern of independence described by Rocour. A large number of companies starting manufacturing operation in the U.S. may have chosen a different organizational set-up; those present in the U.S., but having expanded their operation, may have made organizational changes in preparation for larger investments.

2) Franko's findings.

The second study concerned with the degree of independence enjoyed by U.S. subsidiaries of European companies is that published in two articles by Lawrence G. Franko[e]

This study is in almost complete disagreement with previous findings. It would seem that, on the average, European companies allowed their U.S. subsidiaries no greater freedom than did U.S. companies their foreign subsidiaries. Although Franko does concede that in comparison to Europe's other foreign subsidiaries, U.S. subsidiaries were allowed greater deviation from standard European policies because of the more uncertain competitive environment in the U.S. (17). Moreover, Franko noticed a movement toward greater headquarters involvement both in standardization and guidance of policies (including marketing programs) for U.S. operations (18).

This situates the problem that we intend to research. In the debate over the location of authority in multinationals, knowledge of present practices and the reasons for their existence is essential. Yet, there is a lack of systematic research in this area and *especially* as concerns the kind of control exercised by European firms upon their American subsidiaries. The studies of Rocour and Franko, of course, present important exceptions; however, their findings are at once too purely descriptive and too sharply contradictory to provide a clear and adequate analysis of the situation.

It is our intention to focus on just the area covered by Rocour and Franko but to use an empirical rather than a descriptive method. We hope in this way to come closer to the reality concerning European control of American subsidiaries and thus contribute to a better formulation of the general problem of control on the normative level.

II. Nature and Specifications of the Study

A. Focus of this Research

   If, as we pointed out earlier, control over U.S. operations by European home-offices may have increased since 1962 due to the changes described in the previous section, such an extreme transformation (as that suggested by Franko) in a period of eight years naturally arouses some suspicions. However, we cannot allow an a priori judgment, and must first consider the differences in the methods used by the two researchers to reach their conclusion. This will not be a simple task, because while Rocour does give many details concerning methodology (6), Franko is less explicit (we should keep in mind that the stated purpose of his research is "to explore a number of strategic and administrative alternatives for the management of European companies manufacturing operations in the U.S." (12) and consequently his published findings are directed toward business executives rather than academic circles).

   Nevertheless, from the information available we can point out that whereas Rocour bases his findings on subsidiary executives' responses only, Franko bases his on interviews with "Headquarters and/or U.S. subsidiary managers" of 38 companies and on the partial or full responses of "30 parent or subsidiary managers" to a questionnaire (19). This implies at least that for some companies (we do not know the proportion[f]) only headquarters executives' opinions have been taken into account. If we can expect some systematic downward bias in subsidiary managers' assessment of parent company control, we can similarily expect an upward bias in headquarters' evaluation (It is a human tendency to enhance one's feelings of self worth). In any case this dissimilitude in investigative methods could be one explanatory factor in the discrepancy in the findings.

   A more serious problem is that the companies sampled in the two studies represent a different universe. Rocour included in his sample U.S. companies of all sizes with 50% or more of its stock in the hands of European owners (20) whereas Franko focused primarily on the European companies in the "Fortune 200" list that had equity interests of 25% or more in U.S. manufacturing operation. The consequence of this different choice of universe is that the average size of the first study's parent company was necessarily smaller than in the latter. As we shall point out later in this chapter, it is generally to be expected that the size of the parent company will have an inverse relation to the level of autonomy left to the subsidiary. But most important, Franko makes no attempt to represent the universe of U.S. subsidiaries in his sample and, consequently, one must retain certain reservations with regard to the value of his finding for U.S. subsidiaries in general.

There remains a serious need of reexamining the present situation to find out the general pattern of control exercised by European-based firms on their U.S. manufacturing subsidiaries. The main objective of this present research is to investigate this pattern with a focus on marketing decision. The second purpose of this study is to determine what factors affect the degree of autonomy enjoyed by Europe's U.S. manufacturing subsidiaries as regard marketing decisions. (The two studies mentioned earlier did not really ask: *why* differences occur in the level of control exercised by the parent company over its U.S. subsidiary, although we can reasonably assume that in both studies some variance existed within the group with respect to that variable) . In any case, we believed that a proper evaluation of discriminating ability of such factors could be of use in designing an appropriate scheme of decision-making in multinational corporations.

B. Model for Research: the Main Independent Variables

In order to achieve our second objective we decided to test a certain number of hypotheses suggested by the available literature on organization and control in the multinational company. We indeed believe that with the progress of international business studies in the last fifteen years, an empirical research study based on previous published findings would be more adequate and certainly more enriching than a descriptive study without systematic analysis or testing of hypotheses. Therefore, we consider a set of independent variables found in previous research to be directly related to the level of control exercised by the home-office over the marketing decisions of its subsidiaries. Obviously some of the variables may be interrelated, however we state these hypotheses ceteris paribus (all other things being equal).

1) Technological sophistication of products manufactured.

Firms manufacturing technologically sophisticated products (i.e., requiring large amounts of research and development or engineering inputs in their design or manufacturing process) are expected to exert more control over the subsidiary's marketing decision, because the way in which the products are to be used is highly similar around the world (21). This similarity creates opportunities to apply standards of measurements and evaluations on an international basis.

2) Sensitivity of products to cultural or environmental differences.

In many cases a multinational corporation has to introduce changes in the specifications and characteristics of its products in order to adapt them to a foreign environment for example a legal environment affecting the specification of products such as pharmaceuticals, automobiles...(legal standards being different from one country to another) or culture (taste differences may require modification of the sweetness level for some food products or different styling or color choices for consumer durable goods). It is expected that if the products manufactured by the firm are highly sensitive to these environmental or cultural differences the level of autonomy granted to the subsidiary will be greater than for products less sensitive to these variances. It follows that is should be more difficult to apply international standards for products highly sensitive to environmental or cultural differences, and that in these cases subsidiary managers need higher autonomy in order to accommodate marketing practices to the prevailing situation (21) (22) (23) (24).

3) Size of total corporation.

It was expected that the size of the total corporation (i.e. parent company plus all its subsidiaries and affiliates) would have an inverse relation with the level of autonomy left to the subsidiary. This proposition was based on Brooke and Remmers findings (25). The cause of this relationship according to these authors is that "a close connection across frontiers is clearly expensive and the small company does not have the resources. In the company which does have the resources, on the other hand, this very fact may be an extra pressure to a close relationship. Some of these "resources" in the form of functional staff at head office, will be an active pressure group advocating a closer arrangement. The big company to whom the profit of any individual subsidiary is less important than it is to the small firm, establishes a closer relationship because it can afford it."

4) U.S. subsidiary absolute size.

According to Alsegg (26) one of the most significant factors influencing the degree of autonomy normally granted to local management is the size of the subsidiary. In general a corporation will give more autonomy to a large subsidiary for it probably has the ability to support a full-scale staff. Although Alsegg points out that a very small subsidiary may be left on its own simply because the parent company must devote most of its time to the bigger units, we do not think that this applies to manufacturing subsidiaries but only to some small sales-offices which do not count very much for the parent company. By setting up manufacturing operation, the parent company has already shown a special interest (which required a financial commitment of resources). Therefore we have hypothesized a direct relation between absolute size of the subsidiary and its level of autonomy.

5)   Relative importance of parent company's international operations.

A fairly strong relation was expected to exist between the parent company's share of total sales derived from its international operations and tighter control in local decision-making. This hypothesis is based on Aylmer's findings (1). Indeed, as international operations of the company increase in size, the interest of the parent and therefore its involvement in these operations will be likely to grow in proportion. As a consequence, the firm may well feel the need to support at headquarters a large staff of people knowledgeable about worldwide markets and able to control to a larger extent the subsidiaries' operations (27) (28).

6)   U.S. subsidiary relative size.

It was hypothesized that a direct relation between level of autonomy of a subsidiary and its size relative to the total corporate sales existed. This proposition is based on the Aylmer (1) and Rocour (7) findings. The rationale behind this hypothesis is that control of business activities requires staffing or at least managerial time; the larger the subsidiary, the larger the amount of these inputs needed to control it. The parent company's ability to finance these inputs is generally directly related to its size (see variable 3). Consequently, for parent companies of the same size, the larger the subsidiary the more money required of the parent to control activities and therefore the less likely that the home-office will be able to control the subsidiary. The same reasoning is true the other way around: for subsidiaries of the same size, the larger the parent company's total size the more likely it will have the financial capacity to control the subsidiary. Hence we expect a positive relation between relative subsidiary size and autonomy of decision-making.

Moreover, the human factor plays here too; the managers of a subsidiary which is large in relation with the parent might well feel more powerful and therefore less willing to comply with the home-office directives than the managers of a smaller subsidiary.

7)   Width of range of products provided by subsidiary.

From the findings of Skinner (29), Stopford and Wells (30) and Alsegg (31) follow the proposition that subsidiaries having a wide range of products will tend to be more autonomous than those with few uniform products and markets. Indeed, with a variety of different products it becomes more difficult for the headquarters to exert a direct authority on the marketing decision (The difficulty will increase if these products serve different markets). While, with a narrow line of products, standardization of marketing procedures is much easier and, consequently, headquarters are more strongly motivated to take advantage of this standardization potential by coordinating and controlling these procedures. At the extreme, in firms having acquired strong skill in providing one product or one service to their customer, centralization of marketing decisions on a supranational basis could be relatively easy (32).

8)   Age of subsidiary.

The literature available suggests that a long-established subsidiary is likely to enjoy more autonomy in its decision-making (33) (34) (35), although it has also been found that in the first phase of the subsidiary a high measure of autonomy may be accorded to its manager (36). This may probably be explained by the fact that the foreign investment was small and not too critical for the parent company, which is rarely the case in a production plan investment. Therefore a direct relation between the age of the subsidiary and the level of autonomy it enjoys was expected. The logic of this proposition is that the home-office often assumes that for an older subsidiary most problems have been solved long ago and that there is less need for guidance.

9)   Speed of change in market.

According to numerous findings (37), firms producing lines of products involving mature goods and stable technologies are more likely to centralize decisions at headquarters than those involved in rapidly changing technologies and markets. We indeed expected to find less control exercised over subsidiaries maufacturing products subject to rapid style changes, or needing a heavy flow of new products in order to compete. More generally, we hypothesized that the higher the speed of change in the market, the greater the degree of autonomy left to the subsidiary; a rapidly changing market needs fast answers and fast reactions better handled at the local level, without the delay which home-office intervention would require.

10)   Subsidiary performance.

Acccording to Keegan (39) when a subsidiary fails to achieve budget, the difference between the budgeted and actual performances will trigger intervention from headquarters.   On the other hand, if a subsidiary performs successfully, the headquarters will not feel a need to intervene in its operations.

In general a direct relation between the subsidiary's performance and the level of control exercised by the parent is strongly expected (38).

11)   Motive for investment in the U.S.

The origin of the move to a foreign country by the parent company is often considered to have an impact on the level of autonomy granted to the subsidiary. According to Brooke and Remmers (40), if a company invests abroad to make wider use of its technical lead ("manufacturing strategy"), the subsidiary is likely to be less autonomous than if the company invests to counter threats to the market ("commercial strategy") or in order to achieve geographical diversification ("investment strategy").   In the latter case, if the investment is made through acquisition of an existing company, complete autonomy is frequently retained by the newly acquired subsidiary that continues to manufacture its old product-lines under the former management (41). The explanation given (40) for this relation is that "the technically oriented company which is manufacturing new inventions overseas or is concerned with maintaining a high level of quality is likely to wish to retain a close relationship."   The main headaches of the company will be related to such matters as the protection of patents and trademarks, the maintenance of specification and standards and the constant improvement of the products.   These concerns are not to easily decentralized and whatever form of organization the company devises within it, the relationship will tend to be close. For other types of companies, those described as "commercial" and "investment", these considerations are often less relevant.

These are the findings we proposed to test for European-based U.S. subsidiaries. However, we should at least mention one important factor not accounted for in our scheme of findings. According to some authors (42) (15), some European companies go to the U.S. to learn more sophisticated advertising, marketing and product development techniques to be applied elsewhere by the parent or sister companies. In this case the level of autonomy would, of course, be extremely high; the parent learning from the daughter.

C.   Additional Hypotheses

To the above propositions based on previous research findings surveyed, a number of additional hypotheses were added.

**1)   a) percentage of manufacturing in U.S. for intracompany exports.
b) size of intracompany imports to the U.S. company as compared
to local manufacturing.**

These two variables were expected to be positively related to tight control by headquarters.   Indeed large volumes of intracompany shipments generally indicate a high level of interrelated manufacturing and may therefore probably affect the independence of the subsidiary in all decision areas.

2)   Percentage of ownership.

A positive relationship between percentage of ownership and level of control was expected.   Indeed in cases where the U.S affiliate is part of a joint venture, it becomes more difficult to insert the U.S. company into a global marketing strategy.   (The difficulty will be even greater if the subsidiary is a public company, with local financial reports to be published).

For example, in a subsidiary under full foreign ownership, purchasing its raw materials from the parent, the latter may exert pressure on the subsidiary to increase production and sales even to the point of negatively affecting the subsidiary's profits, while the overall profitability of the total corporation increases.   This type of control is impossible (or at least illegal) when there exists a minority interest.

**3)   Number of countries in which parent company has manufacturing
subsidiaries.**

For any given size of international operations, it seems logical to expect that a firm operating in only a few countries will exercise looser control over subsidiary activities than a company with many subsidiaries in a large number of countries.   In the latter case, it is unlikely that each subsidiary will be able to afford a full-scale local staff to assume complete responsibility for conducting its marketing activities.   Consequently, the home-office will have to create a strong marketing center at headquarters capable of providing the subsidiaries with the management inputs they lack.

Obviously there are a lot of other factors which may affect the level of autonomy of the subsidiary. However, we restricted our hypotheses to those variables which are exogenous to the company's internal organizational policies, because it is only for these that one may establish a priori direction of causality. For example, we could have considered as an additional variable the initiative and independence of the subsidiary's chief executive and hypothesized a positive correlation between this variable and high level of autonomy. However, it would be impossible to assess this variable's direction of causality: (Had the firm first decided to decentralize decisions to the local level and then hired (or kept) a man with these qualities at the head of the subsidiary, or was it because the chief executive of the subsidiary showed independence and initiative that the firm ultimately loosed its control over this subsidiary?). In this case, to designate a priori which was the dependent and which the independent variable would have been mere speculation.

D.   Hypotheses Associated with the Dependent Variables

If we have until now attempted to determine which are the variables likely to influence the level of autonomy enjoyed by the subsidiaries in marketing decisions, we should point out that within marketing, the level of control may vary from one decision area to another.

1)   Control over budgetary versus operational decisions.

According to previous findings (43), the financial decisions are expected to be considerably more controlled by headquarters than other decision areas. This fact has been corroborated in the case of U.S. subsidiaries of European companies by Rocour (7) and Franko (16). Therefore we expected that the budget decisions for marketing activities will be more controlled than the operational or execution decisions.

Budget decisions involve allocation of funds for 1) research and development of new products; 2) marketing research; 3) advertising and sales promotion; 4) distribution, etc.

Operational decisions concern, among other things, 1) policies on distribution channels; 2) pricing; 3) services policies; 4) advertising and sales promotion; 5) packaging, etc.

2)   Control over product-related versus other operational decisions.

Both Wiechman (22) and Aylmer (1) in their studies of U.S.-based multinational corporations pointed out that product policy decisions involved greater degree of headquarters control. This fact may be due to several reasons:

1) Insistance by the home-office on quality standards of the product similar all over the world (failure in that respect in one country may harm the worldwide reputation of the product).

2) Very often product related decisions are associated with capital expenditures (e.g. introduction of a new product line to fulfill the needs of a particular segment of the market) which are likely to be tightly controlled by headquarters.

3) Many companies might think that a great deal of worldwide synergy may be gained in some cases by having a common brand name, or label all over the world. Headquarters might then impose these decisions upon its subsidiaries.

Consequently we hypothesized that the product related decisions (physical characteristics of the product, brand names, packaging and label, product line decisions..) will be more controlled than the other operational decision (pricing, distribution, advertising and sales promotion. . .).

III. Limitations of the Study

1) The study focuses essentially on marketing decisions although the need of investigating the level of control over other areas of business management has also been felt. We tried in most cases to get some insight in some other areas too (finance, manufacturing. . .), but, unfortunately we could not in general conduct in-depth interviews with top executives for all areas of business decisions (due to the executives lack of time).

2) Most of the factors hypothesized have been found related in past studies to subsidiary control in general and marketing decisions control was not always specifically mentioned. Nevertheless, we judged the two were strongly interrelated.

3) Essentially for financial reasons, we limited our sample to companies with headquarters (or at least with an office where key executives were accessible) in the Greater New York area (which includes: New York City, Long Island, Westchester and Rockland counties, Connecticut and New Jersey). This might have introduced a small bias toward centralization (in comparison with other American cities, the frequency of flights from any European city to New York is certainly the highest and the flight fare among the lowest). But we did not think this bias too significant.

4) We only interviewed the subsidiaries managers and never headquarters executives (again because of fnancial constraints). We can for the reason cited above expect consequently a bias toward decentralization in decision-making (although we tried as much as possible, as will be explained in the next chapter, to reduce this bias to minimal dimension). However, we believe that the downward bias (with regard to marketing decisions control) of the subsidiary's executive is certainly less strong than the upward bias we would have found had we interviewed only home-office executives. Indeed we generally think that the subsidiary's management knows better what is going on its own operations than the headquarters management. The subsidiary's manager knows the true situation and therefore the bias downward in terms of control perception have to be a deliberate lie whereas the headquarters executive might not only lie but also be inclined to misinform through ignorance.

Both this limitation and the preceding one should not affect the second objective of our study to determine what factors affect the subsidiary's autonomy for marketing decisions, we had no reason to suspect the biases to be greater for any particular type of company.

5) We did not make a scientific cross comparison with European subsidiaries of U.S.-based companies (again for financial reasons). We had to limit ourselves to the findings of previous studies (which obviously did not use our specific methodology and questionnaire), information gleaned from remarks made during the interviews.

6) In order to allow proper comparisons between companies while keeping the study to amenable dimensions, we only investigated manufacturing subsidiaries, which excludes sales subsidiaries, import offices, trade companies, service industries (finance, insurance, transport. . .) petroleum or mining companies. . . However we included those subsidiaries which only manufacture part of the products they sell and import the rest and those importing new materials or parts and adding value to the product through some manufacturing operation in the U.S.[g]

7) By "subsidiary" we meant any U.S.-based corporation with 50 percent or more of its stocks in the hands of European owners, usually a company. This definition of "subsidiary" is the same as the one given by Rocour (7) which will allow comparisons between the situation in 1962 and in Summer 1975.

8) In this study the corporate hierarchy has been divided only into two levels: "Subsidiary management" and "Headquarters or Home-office management." This latter term refers to any organizational level outside the United States which has the authority to control or otherwise affect the subsidiary's decision.

Conclusion: Purpose and Usefulness of Study

This study will hopefully define more clearly the way U.S. manufacturing subsidiaries marketing decisions are controlled by their European parent. (As was explained before, the previous studies on this subject could not give a proper a priori picture of the situation today). We use a research model which tests the findings of previous research on multinational organization and management as concerns factors affecting subsidiaries autonomy for marketing decisions in the case of European corporate subsidiaries in the United States. To the best of our knowledge this empirical study of the area has never been done before.

Finally, the interest of the executives contacted in the study and the insistance of the vast majority of them on having a report of the findings is one more evidence of the lack of work done on this subject and makes further justification of the contribution of this study unnecessary.

NOTES

[a]For presentation of the divergent viewpoints and a comprehensive bibliography, See: Ralph Z. Sorrenson and Ulrich E. Wiechmann "How Multinationals View Marketing Standardization, *Havard Business Review,* May-June 1975, p. 35.

[b]More details about these variables and studies will be given in the second part of this chapter.

[c]It is difficult for us to see on a priori direct causalty between this "slow historical development" and lack of control.

[d]This also holds for the Department of Commerce publication but to a much smaller extent.

[e]The main findings have been published in 1) L. G. Franko, Strategy + Structure-Frustration = the Experiences of European Firms in American," *European Business,* Autumn '71 pp. 23-42 - 2) L.G. Franko, "European Business Strategies in the United States," Business International S. A. (1971).

[f]We believe (without being able to prove it) from the impression left upon us by the readings of the report and by the way Franko draws his conclusion, that this "proportion" was very high.

[g]In order to provide some further perspective we contacted five sales subsidiaries but they were not included in the study.

REFERENCES

(1)   R.J. Aylmer: "Who Makes Marketing Decisions in the Multinational Firm?" *Journal of Marketing*, vol. 34 (October, 1970), 25-39.

(2)   W.J. Keegan: "Multinational Marketing: The Headquarters Role," *Columbia Journal of World Business*, vol. VI, no. 1 (January-February 1961).

(3)   See R. Buzzel: "Can You Standardize Multinational Marketing?" *Harvard Business Review*, (November, 1968).

(4)   See S. Robock and K. Simmonds: *International Business and Multinational Enterprises* (Richard D. Irwin, Inc., 1973), pp. 457-459.

(5)   See Steward Henderson Britt: "Standardizing Marketing for the International Market, "*The Columbia Journal of World Business*," (Winter, 1974).

(6)   Jean Luc Rocour: "Management of European Corporate Subsidiaries in the United States." (Unpublished Ph.D. dissertation, Cornell University, Septeember 1973.) The main findings have been published in (see below):

(7)   See Jean Luc Rocour: "Management of European Subsidiaries in the U.S.," *Management Internatinal Review* (1966/1).

(8)   See U.S. Department of Commerce Office of Business Economics, *Foreign Business Investments in the United States* by S. Pizer and Z. Warner (Washington D.C. U.S. Government Printing Office, 1962) Table IV.

(9)   See (6) Introduction.

(10)   See Foreign Direct Investors in the United States, List of Foreign Firms with some Interest/Control in American Manufacturing and Petroleum companies in the United States: a United States Department of Commerce Publication 1973.

     See also the "Addendum to the October 1973 list" March 1, 1974.

(11)   J .S. Arpan and David A. Ricks: "Multinational Firms Strategy," vol. 1, Indiana University Bureau of Business Research, Bloomington, Indiana, 1975.

(12)   Jeffrey S. Arpan and David A. Ricks: "Directory of Foreign Manufacturing in the U.S.," Publishing Service Division School of Business Administration, Georgia State University, Atlanta, Georgia, 1975.

(13)   See Robert B. Leftwich: "Foreign Direct Investment in the U.S. in 1973," *Survey of Current Business*, August 1974, Part II.

(14)   See Robert B. Leftwich: "Foreign Direct Investment in the United States 1962-71," *Survey of Current Business*, February 1973.

(15)   L.G. Franko: "Strategy Structure Frustration the Experience of European Firms in America," *European Business*, Autumn 1971, pp. 29-42.

(16)   L.G. Franko: "European Business Strategies in the United States," *Business International S. A.,* 1971.

(17)   See (15) p. 34.

(18)   See (16) p. 40.

(19)   See (16) Preface.

(20)   See (7) p. 13.

(21)   See W. J. Keegan: "Multinational Marketing Control," *Journal of International Business Studies,* Fall 1972.

(22)   See U. E. Wiechman: "Integrating Multinational Marketing Activities," *Columbia Journal of World Business,* Winter 1974.

(23)   See R. J. Alsegg: "Control Relationship between American Corporations and their European Subsidiaries," *A.M.A. Research Study* 102.

(24)   See Yoram Wind, Suzan P. Douglas, Howard V. Perlmutter: "Guidelines for Developing International Marketing Strategies," *Journal of Marketing,* April 1973.

(25)   M. Z. Brooke and H. L. Remmers: "The Strategy of Multinational Enterprise, Organization and Finance," American Elgevier Publishing Company Inc., New York, 1970, p. 88.

(26)   See (23) p. 99.

(27)   See James C. Baker: "Multinational Marketing: A comparative Case Study" in Bernard A. Marin "Marketing in a Changing World, Chicago American Marketing Association," 1969, pp. 61-64.

(28)   W. J. Keegan: "Multinational Marketing Mangement," Prentice Hall, 1974, pp. 525-526.

(29)   W. Skinner: "American Industry in developing economics" John Wiley and Sons, Inc., 1968, p. 191.

(30)   J. M. Stopford and L. T. Wells Jr.: "Managing the Multinational Enterprise/Organization of the Firm and Ownership of the Subsidiaries," Basic Book Inc., New York, 1968, p. 22.

(31)   See (23) pp. 7-8.

(32)   See (4) p. 421.

(33)   See (4) p. 443.

(34)   See (30) pp. 20-22.

(35)   See (23) pp. 100-101.

(36)   See (25) p. 88.

(37)   See (30) p. 22.

(38)   See (23) p. 112.

(39)   See (21) p. 525.

(40)   See (25) p. 72-74.

(41)   See (23) p. 9.

(42)   See S. Robock: "The Silent Invasion."

(43)   See for example R. D. Robinson: "International Business Management, A guide
        to Decision-Making," Holt, Rinehard and Winston, Inc., 1973, p. 587.

        See also Alsegg op. cited (23) p. 7.

CHAPTER 2

METHODOLOGY

I. The Sample

Our sample consisted of fifty-six companies; we considered this an adequate representation of the universe of European manufacturing corporate subsidiaries in Greater New York. What is meant by "Greater New York" and why research results obtained there could be generalized to the rest of the country - this was explained in Chapter I. The companies selected were taken from the list given in the Arpan and Ricks Directory (see *supra* reference (12) of Chapter 1).

We decided to use this list because it was the most recent (at the time of the study) and also because it was possible to overcome its main weakness (the inclusion of a large number of non-manufacturing subsidiaries) by checking through a phone call whether the company was indeed manufacturing (and therefore eligible for inclusion in the universe) or not. On the other hand we had solid grounds to believe that no manufacturing subsidiary was omitted from the list. Indeed the double-checking with the U.S. Department of Commerce publication (see *supra* reference (11) of Chapter 1). Foreign Consulates, Chambers of Commerce, no manufacturing subsidairy was mentioned that did not appear in the Arpan and Ricks Directory.

Seventy companies were contacted through a letter from our thesis director requesting an interview. The letter was generally sent to the chief executive officer of the company in the U.S. Eight companies refused to participate in the study (two replied that their refusal was due to the fact that they were too much solicited for academic studies and had not the manpower to handle them, six replied that it was against the general policy of their company to give any kind of internal information to an outsider). The presidents of five other companies agreed in principle to participate in the study but kept postponing the interview for reasons of lack of time, illness or travel so that we could not include them in this study.

Interviews were finally conducted with executives of fifty-six companies (plus five non-manufacturing subsidiaries not included in the sample). In several cases more than one executive was involved in the interview. In thirty-three cases (about 58% of the companies), the chief executive officer was interviewed. In most other cases a senior executive of the company was the respondent.

II. Data Collection

We considered personal interviews by far the most satisfactory way of gathering our data. An alternative would have been a mail interview but for reasons elaborated below we did not consider it adequate for our purposes. The reasons we considered personal interviews superior to mail interviews were:

1) We could know (in a personal interview) for sure who answered the questions. In a mail interview one has no guarantee that the questions have been answered in a proper way, by a person who understands them properly and who is knowledgeable about the matter involved. In a personal interview, one can sense if the respondent knows what he is talking about, and when he does not know the answer to a specific question, the respondent can then refer the interviewer to another more knowledgeable person. We believe that it is a human trait to find it more difficult to lie or hide the truth from a person sitting in front of you than to write something inaccurate on a questionnaire.

2) A personal interview sometimes gives the respondents an opportunity to think about certain problems that they had never taken the time to consider before but which nevertheless concern them. So, it allows the interviewee to clarify some issues for himself and to exchange ideas with the interviewer. The final result is that the interviewee generally perceives the interview as beneficial. In most cases the respondents even told us that they enjoyed the interview. On the other hand, the respondent benefits less from a written interview and therefore will devote less attention and time to it; consequently one is just that much more uncertain to what degree data gathered this way reflect the truth.

In many cases president of important companies took a few hours of their time to describe in great detail the situation and to discuss the issues involved. This they would never have done in answering a written questionnaire, which most thought "a very boring process." Many of the interviewees told us that they sometimes get requests for written interviews to which they never reply because they do not have the time. It is amazing to think that these executives spent much more time with us than that required to fill out a written interview (even a lengthy one). But, as the senior executive of a very important company pointed out "pure generosity does not exist. By talking and discussing with someone about a certain number of subjects, I also get something out of it."

3) Worries about confidentiality and secrecy are very often strong inhibitors in written interviews. People are somehow much more concerned that a written answer as opposed to an oral one, should

remain confidential. Although except in a few cases, the interviews were all tape-recorded, it did not seem to occur to the respondent that the secrecy of the responses would not be kept. This is certainly due to the fact that in a personal interview one makes the acquaintance of the person who will use the data and somehow one feels more confident that he will keep his word. It follows that we can expect much more openness in a personal than in a mail interview.

Because of the two factors just mentioned (2 and 3), the rate of positive response to requests for mail interviews is generally much lower than we obtained. Consequently relying on mail interviews to make any kind of generalization is likely to result in a very strong statistical bias.

4) By gathering our data through personal interviews it was also possible to get additional comments or explanations which gave a better understanding of the specific situation. As a mail interview must be very limited in scope, one can only get "dry" data which do not always reflect the real facts.

5) It would have been impossible to make an "in-depth" interview through mail. We will explain in the next section why we considered the in-depth interview a crucial means of obtaining the best picture possible of reality.

6) Personal interviewing is the best way to avoid ambiguity in the interview. One can more easily make sure that the respondent understands the question the way it is intended. This method also allows the greater flexibility so badly needed when faced with companies of totally different backgrounds (in terms of size, industries to which they belong. . .) and respondents with different styles and levels of analysis.

In sum we strongly felt that personal interviews were superior to mailed ones, and for that reason we used only the first method to collect our data. The main weakness of a personal interview (response bias that may be introduced when the interviews are conducted by different people who might furthermore have been improperly selected)[a] has certainly been overcome by the fact that there was only one interviewer for all companies.

We generally insisted on interviewing the chief executive officer of the U.S. subsidiary and we generally succeeded in reaching him or at least a knowledgeable senior executive. People farther down the hierarchical scale in the organization do not always have a correct knowledge of the facts; In some instances we had to check answers received at these levels again with the president of the company. In one instance we interviewed the president of a company after having spoken with the head of the marketing department. According to the responses of the latter, all budgetary decisions needed home-office approval. The president of the company told us that this was in fact not true: "This guy, you spoke with, is very nice, but he is a follower, not a leader. He is always asking for directions and thinks consequently that I do the same, which is not true. Indeed I ask him to prepare a very detailed marketing budget, and, in order to strengthen his motivations to do it well, I let him believe that this will be transmitted to the European headquarters, but, take my word for granted, this budget never gets out of my desk."

Except for five cases, all the interviews were tape-recorded. This helped to conduct the interviews in a more relaxed atmosphere, the respondent could speak at his natural speed (because the interviewer does not have to take notes), the interviewer could look into the eyes of the interviewee (rather than at his notebook) which is both more polite, and useful in creating a climate of confidence. All comments and explanations of the interviewee (which very often do reflect the reality in a significantly better way than direct answers to the questions) were recorded. The presence of the tape-recorder microphone is less noticeable than note taking by the interviewer and often tends to be forgotten by the respondent. As a consequence, the respondent may very often "warm-up" and say things he would not have said had he been constantly concerned that his comments could possibly be turned against him.[b] Finally the interviewer can devote full attention to the respondent's talk without worrying about losing any of its substance, which can be integrally reproduced months later at the time of the analysis.

III. Structure of the Interview

The problems we had to deal with in order to measure the independent variables were different than for the dependent ones. Consequently, we are going to explain separately the method used for each set. Generally speaking, except maybe for the "subsidiary's performance" variable, we did not have any particular reason to expect any intentional or subjective bias in the interviewee's answers for the independent variables (problem we had to be prepared to deal with for the dependent variables). Yet, we still had to make sure that the respondent understood the question the way we wanted him to understand it and find a way of measuring those independent variables in order to enable comparisons between companies.

A. Independent Variables

For the *variables related to size*, we could use direct questions, hence we could get ratio scale measure for the variables "U.S. subsidiary absolute size" through question 21^c "size of total corporate" through question 20a; "relative importance of parent company's international operations" through question 20c and "U.S. subsidiary relative size" through questions 21 and 20a. In many cases the answers to some of these questions could be found in the parent company's annual report.

We could use similar ratio scale measurements for the *variables* *"age of subsidiary," "age of subsidiary as a manufacturing entity"* through question 4; "percentage of manufacturing in United States going to intra-company exports" through question 11; "size of intra-company imports to the U.S. company as a percentage of local manufacturing" through question 17; "percentage of ownership" through question 6; "number of countries in which parent company operates" through question 13 and "time of presence of the U.S. subsidiary chief executive officer in his functions" through question 2 or 58 (depending on whether the interviewee was the chief executive officer or not).

To measure the other variables was more complicated and the use of direct questions not necessarily adequate. Consequently for the next variables the interview was loosely structured. Indeed with regard to *"width of range of products provided by subsidiary,"* we could not simply ask: "How many different products do you handle?" Because we could have possibly got as a answer a similar number from a small company manufacturing bolts and from a big multi-divisions firm dealing with many industries. Consequently, we decided to ask the question in the following way: "What are the major products or product groups of your company?" (See question 9). With the help of a catalogue of the company's products generally provided by the interviewee, we could then rank the company on a scale according to the width of products it provided.

In order to measure the variable *"level of performance,"* we first asked question 15 ("How does the home-office evaluate the performance of your company? - Sales, growth, R.O.I., profit after taxes, R.O.S., market share. . .?). Indeed it would have been incorrect to judge the performance of a company on the basis of one specific yardstick if the objectives of the parent companies with respect to their U.S. subsidiary were different. Then we asked questions 16 and 18 which gave us an idea of the outcome. But, essentially we relied on the answer to question 19 generally preceded by a statement: "On the basis of the "yardstick" used by your parent company to judge your performance, is your parent company very satisfied, quite satisfied. . .not satisfied at all with the results of your company?" Hence we tried to make clear to the interviewee that what we were looking for was whether and to what extent a gap existed between where the U.S. subsidiary was and where the home-office thought it should be in terms of performance. If we found abnormal discrepancies between answers in question 16 and 18 on the one hand and question 19 on the other hand, we asked for further explanation before assessing on a scale the level of performance of the subsidiary. (In general and that was true for all questions for which a straightforward answer was not sufficient, we tried to make sure by discussing the issue with the respondent, that he understood the question and that the answer given was accurate).

For the variable *"technological sophistication of the products manufactured"* we used five indirect questions first (25c, 26, 27, 28, 29) which gave the respondent the possibility to give details about the technological aspects of the product. Then came a more direct question in order to enable us to make an ultimate judgement. "In terms of technological sophistication of the product, if I give a rating of 1 to the fashion industry which I believe is at the lowest extreme of the scale and if I give a 10 to the computer or aircraft industry which I believe is at the other extreme of the scale, where would you locate your company in this 1 to 10 scale?" After the respondent gave his opinion, we checked if there was any discrepancy between the rating he gave on this scale, on the one hand, and his answers to the indirect questions and the responses of other interviewees in companies belonging to the same industry, on the other hand. We then further discussed the issue until we clarified it in its entirety in order to enable us to give the proper rating. In cases where the firm manufactured product groups with different levels of technological sophistication, we rated, using the same technique, each of the product groups and multiplied these rating by the relative weight of each of these groups in the overall dollar sales.

For the variables *"speed of change in the market"* and *"sensitivity of the products to cross cultural or environmental differences,"* we proceeded in a similar way. In the first case we asked questions 22, 23, 24 which were indirect questions and then asked a direct question of the type: "In terms of speed of change in the market, if I give a rating of 1 to the steel industry which, I believe, is not at all subject to market changes and makes more or less the same product for a hundred years or so, and if I give a rating of 10 to the fashion industry which would be at the other extreme, where would you locate your company on this one to ten Scale?" We then used the same method as for the variable "technological sophistication of the product" in order to assess a measure for this variable.

For the variable *"sensitivity of the products to cross cultural or environmental differences,"* we used questions 30, 31, and 38 as an indirect way of getting information on the subject, then we asked question 34 as a direct question generally supplemented by a question of the type: "In terms of sensitivity to environmental and/or cultural differences, if I give a rating of one to the steel industry, steel being I presume the same all over the world, and ten to particular items of the food industry like coffee or soups for which specifications have to be drastically changed from one country to another in order to adapt these products to taste differences, where would you locate your company in this one to ten scale with respect to sensitivity to any environmental (legal, climate, economical and/or cultural (color preferences, taste. . .) differences?" Again we used the same method as for the two preceding variables to give an ultimate rating for this variable.

Finally for the variable *"motive of investment in the U.S."* We asked question 10a (a direct free answer question) first, probing thereafter with questions 10b and 10c.

In general we could say that we used a semi-direct, semi-indirect, loosely structured way of interviewing in order to measure the independent variables. The use of direct question was adequate in certain cases (as explained above) but for some other variables we could not have obtained in that way accurate information allowing for measurement. We had to keep in mind that we were dealing with companies from totally different industries and with respondents with different backgrounds and intellectual abilities. Our ultimate objective being to compare the companies on the basis of these independent variables, we did not hesitate to use different wording, add another question, change the order of questions when we felt it was necessary in order to get the most correct measures in a specific set-up. As pointed out above, being the sole interviewer, we avoided the inherent bias existing when comparing non-direct-structured interviews collected by different people.

B.   Dependent Variables

In order to measure the dependent variable, i.e., degree of control exercised by the parent company over its U.S. subsidiary on the different marketing decisions, several alternatives were available.

The first one (which is often used) is to present to the interviewee a semantic differential scale, for each of the decisions investigated, ranging from "no autonomy" or "complete determination by headquarters" to "full autonomy" and to ask him to show the level of autonomy enjoyed by his company in making the specific decision along this predetermined scale.

The main advantage of this method is that it gives very neat quantitative data easily tabulated and susceptible to be analyzed through a great deal of statistical computer packages. However, this method has so many shortcomings that its advantage becomes insignificant. First of all, it is very boring to answer questions set this way. Second, it puts the burden of judging the autonomy on the respondent rather than on the analyst who certainly should have a more objective way of measuring it. Third, the words "autonomy" or "control" do not have the same meaning for everybody. Fourth, the respondent does not generally have any basis of comparison for ranking his company on a one-to-seven or one-to-nine or any dimension semantic scale. This is especially the case when one does not find himself at either extreme of the scale. Therefore, the judgement will be very difficult for the respondent and totally subjective. Fifth, not every marketing decision is important in all cases, for example services policy is certainly not extremely relevant for a chewing-gum manufacturer (we do not know of any chewing-gum producer giving to the final consumer a guarantee on its products). By asking all respondents the same standard questions we would have run the risk of getting a "full autonomy" answer for an item without importance in certain cases, and consequently biased data on the overall. To conclude, we think this method gives data not depicting reality and therefore unfitted to a scientific study.

Another method is to further describe each number in the semantic scale by a statement. For example, we could have asked the questions this way: "For this specific marketing decision, would you say that:

1. The home-office makes the decision alone and imposes it on you, or
2. The home-office makes the decision alone after having sought your advice, or
3. You take the decision at the subsidiary level but you need the home-office approval, or
4. You are primarily responsible but the home-office imposes on you some constraints, or
5. You take the decision totally at the local level.

This method is less conducive to bias than the previous one in that it gives the respondent a basis upon which to make his judgement. However, with this modification, the scale is no longer continuous and statistical analysis assuring continuity in the scale can no longer be used. Besides this, the method has other strong shortcomings as it is too restrictive. It cannot exhaust all eventualities and forces the respondent to choose an alternative which may not always be a reflection of reality. Indeed too many possibilities may occur, in a comparative study of the type we were involved with, which do not allow any exhaustive set of ranked statements going from full autonomy to no autonomy at all, to be established. In fact, if we take the five-statement example given above, which alternative should be chosen by a respondent if, for a certain marketing decision, the home-office makes the decision alone in some cases but in other circumstances leaves full freedom to the subsidiary. Or, if the home-office makes the decision alone for part of the product groups but leaves a free hand to its subsidiary management for the other groups. Or, if headquarters make the decision but will not implement it without the subsidiary's approval. Or, if the decision is generally taken through constant consultation between home-office and U.S. Company. Or, if the parent assists the subsidiary's management in making the decision. . .? We could keep on going with this list but essentially our point is that it is not feasible to exhaust all eventualities.

Between full autonomy of the subsidiary and full control by headquarters, many terms delineating in-between states are hard to rank *a priori* on a scale (for example: assistance, help, direction, guidance, constraints from headquarters; cooperation, coordination, consultation, influence in the policy   making, etc. . .).

We concluded that the best way to measure autonomy (our ultimate objective) was to first get from the respondent what he could do objectively: an accurate description of the process through which marketing decisions were taken in his company. Consequently we tried to have the interviewee describe the situation (as opposed to judging it), in order for *us* to make the evaluation and thereafter comparisons. For that purpose it was necessary to use an in-depth (mostly unstructured) interview. For the marketing operational decision we proceeded in this way:

We started by asking question 43 in order to get an idea of the importance level of each decision The purpose of this question was to spend more time on the important decisions and eliminate questions on non-relevant issues.   Then for each specific marketing decision we questioned the respondent in-depth, the manner of questioning and the order of the questions being adapted to each situation. For example, if we felt that the executive was very defensive and we suspected he wanted to claim more autonomy that his company had in reality, we started with a question like: "Do you ever get any advice or assistance from the home-office in order to make your advertising messages?"   and then we would continue probing until we were satisfied we had obtained a true description of reality - who make the ultimate decision?   What kind of interference, direction, guidance came from the headquarters? etc.   We also double-checked the answers.   For example, if the respondent described his company as totally on its own with respect to pricing decisions we asked (often after having in the meantime spoken about product or advertising decisions):   "Do you have complete latitude for changing the prices of your products?"   Or, at the end of this part of the interview, if the respondent had claimed full autonomy for all marketing operational decisions, we asked: "Would you say that your marketing policies are completely different from those of the parent company?" or

"Don't you have any coordination in the marketing programs between your company and others in the group?"

We also often used indirect ways of getting the information required to measure the variable, like taking a product at random and probing to learn how it was priced and what if any outside influence was at work. (Obviously we could use this method only when the company's products gave way to it, not for a one-product firm, for example). In other cases, we asked another key executive to describe a situation or a process in order to check the first executive's answer especially when the first respondent was not very sure about the way a decision was reached or if we felt that he was speculating rather than describing something he knew).

In sum, we did not leave a subject until we were pretty sure that the information given on that subject reflected the reality.

The operational marketing decisions we insisted upon were:

1.   Pricing (retail, price, trade margin. . .)
2.   Distribution decisions (type of sales force, management of sales force, role of sales force, type of distribution channel, roles of middlemen, type of retail outlets. . .)
3.   Advertising and sales promotions decisions (basic advertising message, creative expression of the message, sales promotion policies, choice of media, media allocation, choice of advertising agency. . .)
4.   Product related decisions
     a.   New product decisions
     b.   Physical characteristics of the product and product specification decisions
     c.   Brand name decision
     d.   Packaging and label decision
     e.   Decisions related to the product line (Adding or dropping a product in an existing product line, adding or dropping a complete product line. . .)

For the other two classes of marketing operational decision: type of market research and services policies (warranty and guarantee policies, after sales services. . .), we only investigated them when relevant. (In some companies for example market research effort is close to nil and considered as unnecessary).

For the budgetary marketing decisions, the questioning was generally a little more direct. We generally used questions such as: "Do you establish a budget in your U.S. company?" "Does the general budget need approval from the home-office?" "What does the budget include?" We were trying to figure out through the questions whether and to what extent the overall budget, the total marketing budget and the different elements of the marketing budget (mainly advertising and sales promotion budget, distribution budget, market research budget) were controlled by headquarters. Question 57 came as an indirect check-back question. If there was any discrepancy between the answer to this question and the information given beforehand we discussed the whole budget issue again in order to avoid any misunderstanding. Finally questions 44, 45, and 50 were (among other purposes) overall marketing decisions checkback questions.

We have already discussed the advantages of using an in-depth interview in order to obtain the least biased data possible relative to other methods of information gathering. We must add that it has other important benefits. First, it is much more agreeable to the interviewee because it allows a flow of conversation instead of the constant constraint of "ranking" on predetermined scales. With the use of scales, the respondent does not have the possibility of explaining what is going on and is often frustrated in his desire to give a proper image of the situation. Second, an in-depth interview gives the interviewee an opportunity to add a lot of pertinent comments and information which threw additional light on different problem areas.[d]

The reader might imagine that, because of all the precautions taken to reduce bias in the data caused by reluctance to admit control by headquarters, the respondents were strongly on the defensive. In fact, that was not generally the case, most of the interviewees were extremely cooperative and anxious to be as accurate as possible in detailing their answers. It is our profound belief that in general we can rely on what they said.

Conclusion

In this chapter we focused on the sample of companies and executives involved in the data collection method used to gather the data and why we chose this method. We did not include in this chapter the way we measured the dependent variable nor the description of hypotheses testing. We found that these explanations fitted more logically in the next chapters. We would like to stress again that the methodology used was considered the best, given that only one interviewer was involved in the process. Had we used a number of interviewers changes in the method would possibly have been necessary.

NOTES

[a]See Paul Green and Donald S. Tull, *Research for Marketing decisions,* 2nd Edition, Prentice-Hall, Inc., 1970, p. 157.

[b]Obviously this would not have been a possibility since we intended to keep our interview confidential as promised. But the respondent could not have, *a priori,* the same basis of certainty.

[c]The questions appear in Appendix C.

[d]These comments were very often the most enriching part of the whole interview, allowing the investigator to really understand and find out what was going on, not only in terms of control but also in terms of the overall relations between the home-office and the subsidiary.

CHAPTER 3

PATTERNS OF CONTROL FOR MARKETING DECISIONS

The purpose of this chapter is to fulfill the first objective of our research, i.e to determine the general pattern of control on marketing decisions exerted by European parent compaines upon their U.S. subsidiaries.

As was explained in the first chapter, it would have been too simplistic to check the level of autonomy for marketing decisions in general. Therefore, having assumed that control might vary among the different classes of marketing decisions, it was considered more appropriate to investigate them individually, according to the methodology detailed in the second chapter, and compare the results between these different decision classes.

I. Operational Marketing Decisons

We explained in the last chapter that we did not want the interviewee to decide what degree of autonomy his company enjoyed for marketing decisions. We rather asked him to describe the process of decision-making, in order for us to evaluate the autonomy level of his company. In order to make an analysis possible, however, some kind of classification had to be made. Consequently, control over each class of operational marketing decisions (pricing, advertising and sales promotion policies. . .) was ranked into five levels depending on the relative amount of autonomy enjoyed by the subsidiary. More specifically, we established five categories of control level and classified each company (on the basis of the description of the situation given the company's respondent) in one of these five categories, each category representing a different level of control measured by the relative participation or interference of the home-office in the decision.

A rating of 1 was given to those cases where the parent company did not exert any influence or interference whatsoever and autonomy was retained by the subsidiary on the specific class of marketing decisions. At the other end of the scale, a rating of 5 was given when the decisions were taken solely by the parent company and imposed on the U.S. subsidiary's management without substantial consultation with him.

A rating of 3 was given when parent company and subsidiary participated more or less equally in the decision, either because the decisions were made through a joint process, or because, although locally taken, they required the parent company's approval, etc. . . A rate of 2 was given when the decisions were "mainly" local; generally were included in this category those cases where although the parent company had exerted some influence on the decisions (through consultation for example) these were ultimately made by the subsidiary. On the other hand we gave a rating of 4 when the decisions were "mainly" made at headquarters level, the typical cases in this category showed the home-office determining policy after having consulted the subsidiary's management.

These five categories were labelled in the following way:

1. Complete Autonomy
2. Large Autonomy
3. Medium Autonomy
4. Large Control
5. Complete Control

The results of the study for each class of operational marketing decisions are shown in Table 1.

An analysis of this table shows that for these decisions in general, U.S. subsidiaries of European corporations enjoy a great deal of autonomy. However, as was hypothesized, product policy decisions involve a greater degree of headquarters control. Indeed, if for pricing, distribution, advertising and sales promotion decisions we found that respectively 92.5%, 89.1% and 82.2% enjoyed complete or large autonomy, the percentage went down to 58.1% for decisions on brand name, 58.5% for decisions on the product line components, 58.8% for new products decisions, 65% for decisions regarding packaging and label and 74% for the physical characteristics of the product.

The general explanation for the small amount of control exerted by headquarters over their U.S. subsidiaries on marketing operational decisions particularly on those non-related to product policies, is that parent company's executives generally think these decisions are better dealt with at the local level.

A. Pricing Decisions

Pricing is generally dictated by the market place and moves by competitors have to be matched quickly. The local management knows better how the market and his customers will react. Consequently, it is generally granted broad autonomy for pricing decisions by headquarters. The general feeling is that headquarters do not know the subsidiary's competitive situation well enough to interfere in this type of decision.

Table 1

Degree of Autonomy Enjoyed for Different Classes of Operational
Marketing Decisions by European Corporation Subsidiaries in the United States

DEGREE OF AUTONOMY

Type of Marketing Decisions	1 Complete Autonomy		2 Large Autonomy			3 Medium Autonomy			4 Large Control			5 Complete Control			TOTAL	
	No. of Cases	%	No. of Cases	%	Cumul. Freq.	No. of Cases	%	Cumul. Freq.	No. of Cases	%	Cumul. Freq.	No. of Cases	%	Cumul. Freq.	No. of Cases	Fre-quency
Pricing	43	81.1	6	11.3	92.5	2	3.8	96.2	0	0	96.2	2	3.8	100	53	94.6
Distribution Decisions	48	87.3	1	1.8	89.1	5	9.1	98.2	1	1.8	100	0	0	100	55	98.2
Advertising & Sales Promotion Decisions	40	74.1	6	11.1	85.2	5	9.3	94.4	1	1.9	96.3	2	3.7	100	54	96.4
New Product Decisions	26	51.0	4	7.8	58.8	11	21.6	80.4	7	13.7	94.1	3	5.9	100	51	91.1
Physical Characteristics of the Product(s)	29	58.0	8	16.0	74.0	4	8.0	82.0	6	12.0	94.0	3	6.0	100	50	89.3
Brand Name	22	51.2	3	7.0	58.1	8	18.6	76.7	5	11.6	88.4	5	11.6	100	43	76.8
Packaging & Label	25	56.8	4	9.1	65.9	8	18.2	84.1	3	6.8	90.9	4	9.1	100	44	78.6
Product Line	25	47.2	6	11.3	58.5	14	26.4	84.9	6	11.9	96.2	2	3.8	100	53	94.6
Market Research Operational Decisions	27	93.4	0	0	93.4	1	3.4	96.8	0	0	96.8	1	3.4	96.8	29	51.7

B.   Distribution Decisions

For decisions linked to distribution policies, it seems that, in general, European home-office executives have trouble understanding the structures of distribution in the U.S. The complexity of the market for distribution channels and systems is greater in the United States than in Europe. Quite typical are the comments of two respondents from different industries: 1) "Our home-office has very little understanding of the American market which is very complex. In fact, our home-office may more easily visualize the Japanese market than the U.S In this country our products are sold by 6000 representatives belonging to 500 different wholesale organizations. The wholesaler, who has a very marginal role in our industry in Europe has been protected by the law in the U.S. and is a crucial element of distribution in this country. This makes the whole distribution policy different than in Europe". 2) "In the home-country the company deals with 250,000 retail outlets, whereas here we deal with a few accounts because there are chain stores. The thing that our sales force has to do here is merchandizing which is unheard of in Europe. In Europe the only thing you ask from a salesman is to sell, to smile, to be nice. . . therefore supervision of distribution policy by headquarters is impossible".

Because of the types of distribution structures in the U.S., the different functions and importance of middlemen and retail institution, it is often difficult for headquarters to monitor these activities, therefore home-offices' executives do not generally get involved in distribution decisions.

C.   Advertising and Sales Promotion Decisions

As concerns advertising and sales promotion decisions, there is in general a recognition of the differences between markets and the need to adapt the advertising messages, their creative expression, the choice of media and the other elements of advertising and promotion programs to the United States. In fact even the approach to advertising differs to a certain extent between European countries and the U.S. For example, a cosmetic company uses billboard ads in France where this type of advertising works quite well, while in the United States the subsidiary of this company does not because it is necessary (according to the company's respondent) "to tell a story first off, to set a mood in the ad in order to make it effective; although women possibly think the same way all over the world with regard to perfumes, what will attract the attention of a U.S. magazine reader or radio listener is not necessarily the same as will attract the attention of her French counterpart."

In most cases, the advertising executional policies were completely different in the U.S than in the country where the parent company was based. Moreover, as the United States are still considered leaders in advertising designs, better resources for effective advertising and sales promotions can generally be found locally and headquarters usually feel that it is wiser to leave these decisions to their subsidiary. However we have to notice that compared to pricing and distribution decisions, where the results show the highest rate of complete autonomy, in quite a few cases, European headquarters try to influence or at least give some advice to their subsidiaries with respect to advertising and sales promotion policies. Some companies even like to have some of their advertising messages standardized worldwide, others push their U.S. affiliate to take a serious look at what has been done elsewhere in order to see if there is some way to take advantage of it. Others insist on having a common basic message worldwide although they leave their subsidiary complete freedom with respect to the creative expression of the advertising message, the choice of an appropriate agency, etc. . . We could conclude from the data that in contrast with pricing and distribution policies where a majority of the companies felt they should not interfere with their subsidiary; for advertising and sales promotion policies the feeling that some kind of worldwide standardization was desirable, or that the parent company's experience could be helpful for its subsidiary was more often found.

D.   Market Research Decisions

In the overwhelming majority of cases, market research operational decisions, when formal market research studies are conducted, are not controlled at all by headquarters. But because a large number of the companies involved in the study did not consider market research an important class of decision, we will not pursue this analysis any further.

E.   Services

In only a limited number of firms decisions services policies were considered important, consequently here again we did not think it appropriate to give this class of decisions further analysis. In any event, there were no cases where any interference or influence whatsoever was exercised from headquarters for those policies. They were completely determined by the local management.

F. Product Related Decisions

The data show that although in these decision areas most subsidiaries still enjoy a great deal of autonomy, there is definitely more interference from headquarters for decisions regarding product policies than for other operational decisions. A few reasons were given as explanation.

First of all, policies related to new products are often associated with some kind of financial investments, an area over which home-offices are generally likely to have more control. Moreover changes in the product line offered to the customer may affect the financial returns of the subsidiary which is also something headquarters like to exert some influence on before any important decision is taken in those respects. In general everything related to financial returns or expenditures is more closely monitored by headquarters, it is therefore not surprising to see that typically home-office executives are more actively involved in those areas.

Another reason for the greater involvement of parent companies in subsidiary product policies is that they are often more knowledgeable than their subsidiaries in this field. Most U.S. affiliates do not have basic research centers, and consequently most of the innovations come from the parent company. Sometimes the U.S. subsidiary will duplicate products already sold in Europe; in these cases home-office executives feel that their prior experience allows them to interfere with subsidiary policies.

In dealing with their U.S. daughter, parent companies are more at ease on the subject of product policies than on what concerns pricing, distribution or sales promotions and advertising decisions. For these latter the local market is the main dictator and most companies feel that any interference would be detrimental to the sale objectives of the subsidiaries. For product policy decision headquarters' executives feel much better equipped to direct their subsidiary. Moreover, if many firms are ready to accept different promotional policies in different countries, some are much more reluctant to see important changes in product formulas or characteristics from one country to another. There is in fact often a clear insistance by the home-office that quality standards for products be uniform worldwide (the weakness of one subsidiary in this regard could hurt the product reputation in the countries).

We have also to keep in mind that European firms are often still more manufacturing-oriented, than marketing-oriented. European home-offices will therefore be more likely to get involved in decisions related to the product rather than to its promotion.

Another factor behind the lower level of autonomy in product related marketing decisions is, in certain cases, the dependence of the various branches on a single production center for parts. The fact that the U.S. affiliate is dependent on the parent company for its raw materials may also seriously restrict autonomy.

Finally, while stopping short of worldwide standardization for advertising or promotion policies, some companies may find the adoption of a common brand name, logo or label feasible and advantageous; consequently they will be likely to restrict their subsidiary's freedom in these areas.

II. Marketing Budgetary Decisions

As for operational decisions we had to classify the companies into different categories according to the level of autonomy they enjoyed for their marketing budgetary decisions. The respondents' answers showed that the control level exercised by headquarters over budgetary marketing decisions was not different from one marketing decision to another. For example, policies of control were generally the same for budgetary decisions related to distribution as those related to advertising. There existed an overall pattern of control over budgetary matters with certain consequences for autonomy of budgetary decision in marketing. Therefore, it seemed more appropriate to give a general rating for the level of control on marketing budget policies rather than to rate each class of decision individually. Moreover, it became quickly obvious that a different kind of classification had to be devised than that used for operational decisions since control over budgetary decisions was exerted in a different way. In contrast with operational decisions the questions of worldwide standardization does not often arise. Although there may be standard procedures or standard reporting systems within a multinational corporation, there is no real standardization of marketing budgetary decisions (according to the sense given in chapter 1). Such standardization would mean an attempt to establish identical marketing budgets for subsidiaries of different sizes and with different problems and opportunities. This kind of policy would not, in general, suit the profit or sales maximization objectives of a firm. Even when there does exist control over budgetary decisions, it is of quite a different sort than that exercised over executional policies. The most appropriate basis of classification would be the extent of autonomy a subsidiary enjoys to establish and change, during the course of a year, budgetary decisions without having to consult or await approval from headquarters. For this purpose we established a six-rank scale corresponding to six levels of control exercised over the subsidiary by the parent company.

In the first category were included those cases where the subsidiary presented no budget to the parent company; all budgetary decisions were made internally.

In the second category, were included those cases where the subsidiaries presented an "overall" budget, showing essentially the "top" and "bottom" (sales and net profit) lines, but giving no details for marketing expenditures. For this category, there was no interference nor was approval necessary for the size of marketing expenditures.

In category three, were included those companies where detailed marketing expenditures were expressed in the budget submitted to the parent company, making them subject to discussion and comments from headquarters' executives. However, subsidiary's executives were free to increase (or decrease) these expenses during the course of a year without having to refer to headquarters in so far as sales and profits were not negatively affected.

In the fourth category, were included cases where the entire budget, with its detailed marketing expenditures, was not only discussed with headquarters' executives but also required their approval. Only marginal increases in the marketing budget (generally no more than 10% could be made during the course of the year by the subsidiary's executives without prior approval by headquarters.

In category five, were included those cases where once again the entire budget, with detailed marketing expenditures, had to be discussed with headquarters or necessitated their approval. No increase in the overall marketing expenses budgeted could be made during the course of a year without first obtaining headquarters' approval. However, the shifting of allocated resources from one marketing activity and another (for example from distribution to advertising) was allowed without prior approval from headquarters.

Finally in the sixth category were included those cases where all marketing expenses were expressed in detail in a budget requiring approval of headquarters and where no non-budgeted money could be spent during the course nor any shift of allocated resources made without prior approval from the home-office.

The distribution of cases for each category of control level are shown in Table 2.

Comparing the results shown in Table 2 with those of Table 1, one can see that the level of control exerted by headquarters on their U.S. subsidiaries is generally higher for budgetary decisions than for operational decisions. While for operational decisions involving distribution, advertising and sales promotion from 89.1% to 85.2% of the companies were largely autonomous, only 42.9% of the companies had the same degree of autonomy as concerns the marketing budget. Even if we consider the companies classified in category three as fairly autonomous since they might increase marketing expenditures during the course of a year without prior permission of headquarters, it still remains that 39.3% of the companies (those classified in categories 4, 5, & 6 for budgetary decision) could not make substantial changes in their marketing budgetary policies without prior approval from home-office.

Table 2

Degree of Autonomy Enjoyed by European Corporate
Subsidiaries in the United States for Marketing Budgetary
Decisions

	Number of Cases	Frequency	Cumulative Frequency
Category 1	15	26.8%	26.8%
Category 2	9	16.1%	42.9%
Category 3	10	17.9%	60.7%
Category 4	4	7.1%	67.9%
Category 5	7	12.5%	80.4%
Category 6	11	19.6%	100.0%
T O T A L	56	100	100.0

The data then confirm the hypothesis, stated in Chapter 1, that budget decisions for marketing activities were more likely to be controlled than operation decisions.   Indeed, we frequently heard comments like the following: "Once the budget is approved, we can make whatever advertising or distribution policies we want. For example we can choose the advertising media or channels of distribution we find the most adequate. But if a decision involves an increase in expenses then we have to refer to headquarters for approval" or "The marketing budget is closely checked and controlled by our parent company, but the way we use those funds is up to us."

This tendency to control budgetary decisions more closely than operational decisions (especially the non-product related ones) is quite typical of a certain number of companies, and most respondents assessed a much higher level of headquarters' involvement in all areas connected with finance.[a]

We can advance at least two reasons for this deeper involvement by home-offices in budgetary policies as compared with operational policies. First of all, it is perhaps easier for headquarters to control budgetary decisions as opposed to operational ones which sometimes involve concepts foreign to the parent companies.

Second, many firms see their subsidiary mainly as an investment expected to give a good return. Headquarters' executives leave the subsidiary free to manage the business because they feel that the subsidiary's executives are better placed to do so. However they do want to make sure that their investment will give appropriate returns. Consequently they tend to be more or less closely involved in the financial aspects of the business. Some will only want to check the forecasted sales and profit figures for the year and leave their subsidiary's management a free hand on how to acheive it. Others go as far as to discuss the budget in detail and check each specific item.

A close control over budgetary decisions necessarily has a very serious negative impact on the autonomy of the subsidiary for operational decisions as well. Constraints on the marketing budget must imply certain restrictions on the freedom of decision over marketing programs or policies. This holds even if within the budget the subsidiary is free to make shifts in allocated funds. At the extreme, a very close control on budget would mean almost total restriction of the subsidiary's freedom in managing its marketing operations independently.

The following comments of one of the executives interviewed are typical of this kind of situation: "For operation decisions like pricing, advertising messages, etc., we are on our own, but we have to submit a budget to the parent company which has to be discussed and approved in all its details. We give our suggestions but those have to be approved. In fact, whatever touches finance is highly controlled. To that extent our marketing decision autonomy is clearly affected, for any important marketing decision involves spending funds."

Conclusion

From the findings described in this present chapter, we can conclude that the patterns of control exercised by European parent companies over their U.S. subsidiaries are not atypical in terms of the relative autonomy granted to subsidiaries for different classes of marketing decision. As was hypothesized on the basis of previous research, control is stronger for product-related and budgetary decisions than for product promotion decisions (pricing, advertising and sales promotion policies, distribution policies).

The question of whether the overall pattern of autonomy for marketing decisions is significantly different in the case of European companies operating in the United States than for U.S. companies operating abroad still remains open. In order to answer such a question, a comparative study using the same methodology would be necessary. Without it we can only rely on comments from respondents and other witnesses who have been involved in both situations (i.e. in U.S. companies operating abroad and European companies operating in the U.S.) or on other studies using a different methodology[b] to draw a speculative conclusion. Those sources indicate that European companies in the U.S. would enjoy relatively more autonomy than U.S. subsidiaries in Europe with respect to all decisions in general and marketing decisions in particular.

Some of these sources argue that European companies leave more autonomy to their subsidiaries in general, and not only to their subsidiaries in the U.S. Many of the respondents did not think that their parent company policies were different for the U.S subsidiary than for other subsidiaries.

Some reasons were given to explain why European companies would exert less control on their overseas subsidiaries than U.S. companies do.

1) Many European companies would be understaffed at the top executive level relative to U.S. companies, therefore not enough managerial attention and time can be given to the subsidiaries; as a consequence control on decision is lower than in American multinational corporations.

2) European companies would have more experience in terms of overseas operations. Many of them were already exporting at a time when most American companies were satisfied with the huge local markets at their disposal. Before modern telecommunications were developed, many European companies were alreaady exporting a large proportion of their production and were establishing sales subsidiaries overseas because their own local markets were too small. Because of the lack of rapid telecommunication, most decisions had to be taken at the local level. Delegating decision-making powers to the local management would therefore be (according to this explanation) a long time tradition for European companies. On the other hand, American companies have only recently started to establish themselves overseas and at a time when distances are spanned by rapid communications. They consequently have not found it necessary to decentralize authority and therefore have not developed the European tradition of delegating authority.

3) Another explanation given was that the American multinational corporation's tendency to control may stem from the fact that, when they expanded after World War II, the overseas markets were very small (at least in terms of purchasing power) compared to the U.S.

market. At that time everybody thought American marketing was far
superior to that of most other countries.   American multinational
corporations found it more practical and economical to give strong
directives to their subsidiaries and to take full advantage of potential
synergies in worldwide standardization of marketing policies.   This
situation would have created the tradition of strong control by U.S.
headquarters of overseas subsidiaries which is still alive today.

Some opinions however put forth that the U.S. subsidiary enjoys
greater autonomy than other subsidiaries of the same European company.
The reasons generally given for this privileged situation were:

1) **Size:** In many cases the size of the U.S. subsidiary may be
   very important and the subsidiary can then afford an
   adequate staff to make its own decision. As will be shown in
   the next chapter, size being a factor of autonomy for
   marketing decisions, this explanation my be satisfactory.
2) **Distance:** The greater distance between U.S. and Europe than
   between one European country and another was sometimes
   considered as a factor for the relative autonomy of the U.S.
   subsidiary.   Indeed, although modern communications have
   greatly reduced distances, it still remains that it is easier and
   especially cheaper to control a subsidiary located a few
   hundred miles away from headquarters than one located
   thousands of miles away.   Control involves not only
   intervention of top management but also lower level
   executives or staff. Continual travel and communication back
   and forth from Europe to U.S. may be too heavy an expense
   for some firms, which would then leave their U.S. subsidiary
   quite on its own.
3) **Feeling of Incompetency in the American Market:** In some
   companies, headquarters executives feel incompetent to
   interfere in their U.S. subsidiary's activities. It has already
   been stated that the American distribution set-up is difficult
   to be clearly visualized by many European headquarters. For
   some this difficulty does not stop at the distribution level, the
   whole American market and competitive situation is much
   more unfamiliar to them than other European markets. As a
   consequence, they may leave their U.S. subsidiary on its own,
   looking at it more as an investment than as an affiliate.

NOTES

[a]Of all business decisions, those related to capital expenditures were found to be the most closely controlled by parent companies.

[b]See for example conclusions of U.E. Wiechman, "Integrating Multinational Marketing Activities," *Columbia Journal of World Business*, Winter 1974, pp. 9-10.

CHAPTER 4

FACTORS INFLUENCING THE DEGREE OF CONTROL FROM PARENT COMPANIES ON U.S. SUBSIDIARY'S MARKETING DECISIONS

I. Impact of the Independent Variables

The objective of this chapter is to fulfill the second goal of our research: to determine what factors affect the degree of autonomy enjoyed by U.S. manufacturing susidiaries of European companies for marketing decisions. For that purpose we considered a set of independent variables that previous research found related directly to the level of control exercised by the home-office over its subsidiaries' marketing decisions. Details of the hypotheses have been given in Chapter 1.

All the hypotheses have been tested except for the relation between motive of the investment in the U.S. and the level of control exercised by the parent companies. The reason for this omission is that almost without exception the parent company invested in the U.S. primarily as a commercial or investment strategy. It would therefore have been futile to test the hypothesis that a subsidiary is likely to be less autonomous when the motive for investment is manufacturing strategy since this, in fact, was seldom the case.

In order to test the fourteen other hypotheses we had to take into account the fact that since the dependent variables (the various levels of autonomy for each marketing decision) were measured on an ordinal scale, nonparametric statistical tests had to be used in order to test the hypotheses. One of them, the Spearman's r_s correlation coefficient was found appropriate for our purposes.[a]

Appendix D shows for each of the postulated factors the Spearman's r_s correlation coefficient between this factor and the subsidiary's level of autonomy measured for each class of marketing decision. It also shows the correlation's significance level (the probability that the observed value of the correlation coefficient differs from zero only by chance). We did not show the correlation coefficient whenever the significance level was higher than 15%.[b]

Before proceeding to the analysis of the results for each of the factors postulated as having an impact on the autonomy of the subsidiary on marketing decisions, we remind the reader that the level of autonomy for each marketing decision class (dependent variable) was measured in such a way that a higher value given to the variable meant a higher level of control (details on the classification procedures were given in Chapter 3). For the independent variables or postulated factors, they were ranked in a way such that when a firm scored higher on the variable, the rank given was higher too. The exceptions to this rule were the three variables "sensitivity of the products to cultural or environmental differences," "speed of change in the market" and "subsidiary performance" where when a firm scored higher on the variable, the rank it was given was lower.

All the independent variables were interval-or-ratio-scaled following the method explained in Chapter 2.

A.   Technological Sophistication of Products Manufactured

The results did not show evidence that the subsidiary's level of autonomy decreased when the technological sophistication of the products manufactured increased. We could not reject the null hypothesis (that no relation exists) for any marketing class at any level of signifiance between 5% and 15%.

B.   Sensitivity of Products to Cultural or Environmental Differences

For decisions having to do with: pricing, advertising and sales promotion, new products, physical characteristics of products, brand name, packaging and labels and product line, we could reject the null hypothesis at a 5% level of significance. For the other decision classes we could not reject the null hypothesis at a 5% level of significance. However, we could do so at a 10% level for decisions concerning distribution and at a 12.6% level for those involving marketing budgets.

The results show then that the level of control on the subsidiary's marketing decision decreases when the sensitivity of the products to cultural or environmental differences increases. This is particularly true for operation decisions. Therefore in firms dealing with products which are highly sensitive to these differences, the parent company will be more likely to grant a high degree of autonomy to its subsidiary on operational decisions. The correlation is, however higher for product-related decisions because these areas are generally the most closely controlled of all operational decisions. Therefore the difference in degree of control exercised by the parent companies over firms whose products are highly sensitive to cultural and environmental differences will be more marked.

C.   U.S. Subsidiary Absolute Size

For decisions concerning new products, brand names, product line and marketing budgets, we could reject the null hypothesis at a 5 percent level of significance; this was not the case for other decisions. However, the null hypothesis could be rejected for decisions on pricing at 6.2 percent; on physical characteristics of the product at 10.2 percent and on operational decisions at 13.6 percent. Only in the case of decisions involving advertising and sales promotion could the null hypothesis not be rejected at any level of significance between 5 and 15 percent. In fact the results substantiate our expectations that the level of control would decrease as the size of the U.S. subsidiary increased.

D.   Size of Total Corporation

The null hypothesis could be rejected at a 5 percent level of significance for decisions regarding pricing, advertising and sales promotion, new products, brand names and product line. The null hypothesis could not be rejected at this level for the other decisions. However, we could reject it at a 5.2 percent level for physical characteristics; a 6.5 percent level for packaging and labels; a 10.4 percent level for marketing budgets and a 11.9 percent level for distribution.

It would seem then that a link does exist between size of the total corporation and the level of control the parent company exerts on its subsidiary for marketing decision. However, contrary to what was expected, the subsidiary's control over its marketing decisions increases with the size of the total corporation while the inverse proportion had been hypothesized.

Since the variables "size of total corporation" and "U.S. subsidiary absolute size" were strongly correlated, we wanted to check how this related to the positive correlation between autonomy in marketing decisions and "size of total corporation." To this purpose, we compared the Kendall rank correlation coefficient relating "size of total corporation" to degree of control with the Kendall partial rank coefficient linking "U.S. subsidiary absolute size" to its relevant variables. However, the results rendered no novel information.

E.   Relative Importance of Parent Company's International Operations on the Basis of Our Findings

Except for pricing decisions, we could not reject the null hypothesis (that no relation exists between the relative importance of the parent company's international operation and the U.S. subsidiary's autonomy in marketing decisions) at any level of significance between 5% and 15%. For pricing decisions we could reject the null hypothesis at a 6% level of significance.

F.   U.S. Subsidiary Relative Size

The hypothesis that control over marketing decisions of the subsidiaries is negatively correlated with the subsidiary's relative size is not proven by the results for operational decisions. (The null hypothesis could not be rejected at any level of significance between 5% and 15%). However the results show a negative correlation significant at a 8.9% level between the relative size of the subsidiary and the control exerted by the parent company on marketing budgetary decisions.

G.   Width of Range of Products Provided by Subsidiary

For decisions concerning new products, brand names and product line, the null hypothesis could be rejected at a 5 percent level of significance. This was not possible for the other decisions. However, it could be rejected at 5.1 percent level for packaging and label, a 6 percent level for pricing and a 10.7 percent level for physical characteristics. The null hypothesis could not be rejected at any level of significance betwen 5 percent and 15 percent for decisions concerned with distribution operations, advertising and sales promotion and marketing budgets. In general, on the basis of these findings, we can assess that, for most marketing decisions, as the subsidiary's range of products widens its level of autonomy also increases.

H.   Age of Subsidiary

We could not reject the null hypothesis for any of the decisions at a 5 percent level of significance. However, it could be rejected at a 5.3 percent level for pricing (indicating that for this type of decision autonomy increases with age). The null hypothesis could also be rejected for marketing budget decisions at a 9.4 percent level and for brand name decisions at a 11 percent level.

I.   Speed of Change in Market

The Table shows that for most marketing decisions a significant correlation exists between the level of autonomy enjoyed by the subsidiary and speed of change in the market. We could reject the null hypothesis for pricing decisions at a 5 percent level of significance but for the other decisions it could not be rejected at this level. However, it could be rejected at a 6.5 percent level for brand name decisions, at a 7.1 percent for decisions on packaging and labels, at 7.8 percent for those regarding advertising and sales promotion, 8.1 percent for physical characteristics and 12.3 percent for product line.

As was expected less control is exercised over these marketing-decision classes where subsidiaries manufacture products subject to rapid style changes or needing a heavy flow of new products in order to compete. We will note that the positive sign of the correlation coefficient is due to the fact that, as we explained before, the variable "speed of change in the market" like "sensitivity of the products to cultural or environmental differences," and "subsidiary performance" was ranked in such a way that the higher the firm scored on this variable, the lower the value assigned on it.

J.   Subsidiary Performance

It was hypothesized that a subsidiary's autonomy would correlate with its performance. The null hypothesis could be rejected at a 5 percent level for brand name decisions but not for the others. However, it could be rejected at a 6.5 percent level for decisions concerning new products and at 11 percent for those concerning distribution operations.

K.   Percentage of Manufacturing in U.S. for Intracompany Exports

For decisions on distribution operations and marketing budgets, the null hypoyhesis could be rejected at a 5 percent level of significance. This was not possible for the other classes of decisions. However, it could be rejected at a 6.5 percent level for packaging and label decisions, and at a 13 percent level for new products decisions. It seems therefore that a link does tend to exist between the percentage of manufacturing for intracompany exports done in the U.S. and the degree of control exercised by the parent company over its U.S. subsidiary. However, contrary to our hypothesis, the level of autonomy of the subsidiary increases along with the increase of the percentage of manufacturing done in U.S. for intracompany export.

L.   Size of Intracompany Imports to U.S. as Compared to Local Manufacturing

We could reject the null hypothesis at a 5 percent level of significance for decisions regarding distribution operations, new products, product line and marketing budgets. This was not possible for the other decisions. However, the null hypothesis could be rejected at a 13.4 percent level for pricing decisions. As hypothesized, then, the control exercised by the parent company on its U.S. subsidiary for most marketing discussions increases with the increase of the size of intracompany imports to the U.S.

M. Percentage of Ownership

As expected it was found that the percentage of ownership of the subsidiary by the European parent is generaly related to the autonomy of the subsidiary for most marketing decisions. (The higher the percentage of ownership, the higher will the extent of control exerted by the parent company.)

For decisions regarding new produccts, brand names, and product line, the null hypothesis could be rejected at a 5 percent level of significance. This was not the case for the other decisions. However, one could reject the null hypothesis for the following decision classes at the levels indicated: packaging and labels at 7.7 percent, pricing at 11 percent, physical characteristics at 11.3 percent and distribution operations at 14.5 percent.

N. Number of Countries in which the Parent Company has Manufacturing Subsidiaries

We could reject the null hypothesis at a 5 percent level of significance for decisions touching pricing, distribution, new products, brand names, and product line. For the others this was not possible. However, the null hypothesis could be rejected for decisions on packaging and labels at a 9.7 percent level, and at 10.4 percent for those concerning marketing budgets.

However, although it was expected that as the number of manufacturing subsidiaries increased so would the control exerted by the parent company in general and on the U.S. subsidiary in particular, the results show quite the opposite effect: i.e., as the number of countries in which the parent company has manufacturing subsidiaries increases so does the level of autonomy granted to the U.S. subsidiary for marketing decisions.

II. Discriminating Power of the Postulated Factors

Having investigated how each of the factors taken alone affects the subsidiary's level of autonomy and tested the original hypotheses, the next stage of the analysis is to see how, for each of the marketing-decision classes investigated in our study, a combination of these factors can discriminate between different levels of subsidiary autonomy. This will also allow us to check how these factors affect the subsidiary's autonomy for marketing decisions, other things being equal.

For that purpose, two different types of stepwise discriminant analyses were undertaken for each of the marketing-decision classes.

In the first analysis we wished to find out how the factors were able to discriminate between all five (six in the case of marketing budgetary decisions) categories of autonomy.

In the second analysis, we reduced the number of categories of autonomy to two: high and low. In the first category included the cases in which the subsidiary enjoyed "complete" or "wide" autonomy for a specific marketing-decision class. All other cases were grouped in the second category. For marketing budgetary decisions, in the "high autonomy" category were included the cases previously rated as belonging to categories 1, 2, and 3 while the other cases were included in the "low autonomy" category.

In the first analysis we will then first find which variables best discriminate between the groups and how well they predict whether a firm will belong to the correct category. However, this analysis cannot show to what extent each of these discriminating variables has a positive or negative effect on the subsidiary's autonomy when combined with other variables. This is the main purpose of the second analysis, to show which variables are the best discriminators between low and high autonomy and whether their effect on the subsidiary's autonomy is positive or negative.

The stepwise selection criterion used to select the variables was meant to minimize the Wilks' Lambda.[c] The appendix will show for each class of marketing decision the variables selected, the standardized discriminant function coefficient, and the Wilks' Lambda, for which a test of significance is given. We will also show the percentage of cases correctly classified by the discriminant function and compare this result with the "percent correctly classified by chance".[d]

If the percentage correctly classified is higher than the percentage classified by chance, this is further evidence that the discriminant functions and factors are valid. In the multigroup analysis we will also show the given value of the discriminant functions which denote the relative ability of each function to separate the groups.

In the two groups analysis, the centroids summarizing the groups location in the space defined by the discriminant function will be shown. These centroids will not be shown in the multigroup analysis, since they are generally not set in an orderly way and therefore the direction of the effect of the selected variables on the level of autonomy of the subsidiary cannot be assessed.

A. Pricing Decisions

Multigroup analysis (Table I, Appendix E)

The discriminant functions derived from the analysis separate significantly between the groups of different autonomy level.

The variables selected in the stepwise procedure are: "technological sophistication of the products manufactured," "sensitivity of the products of cultural or environmental differences," "relative importance of the parent company's international operations," "width of the range of products provided by the subsidiary," "subsidiary performance," "percentage of manufacturing in United States for intracompany exports."

These variables in their linear combintion are good predictors of the autonomy group to which a subsidiary should belong for pricing decisions, since the percentage of cases correctly classified is higher than the proportional chance criterion and the Wilks' Lambda is quite significant.

Two groups analysis (Table II Appendix E)

As can be seen from the centroids of groups in reduced space figure, the higher a firm scores on the discriminant function, the better its changes of belonging to group 2 (the low autonomy group).

The factor contributing the most to the discriminant function is subsidiary performance (0.69907). Recalling that the higher the score a firm "gets" on this variable, the lower its performance, this shows that the better a subsidiary performs, the lower its chances to belong to group 2. This result is in agreement with what was expected from our original hypotheses. The second contributing factor is speed or change in market (0.60030). Again recalling the higher the speed of change in its market, the lower the firm scores on this variable, the positive sign of the coefficient shows then that, as expected, a firm will be likely to be less controlled by its parent company on pricing decisions (higher chance to belong to class 1) if it manufactures products subject to rapid change, or if it needs a heavy flow of new products in order to compete.

The third contributing factor is percentage of manufacturing U.S. for intracompany exports (-0.45858). Its negative sign shows that as the U.S. subsidiary's percentage of manufacturing for intracompany exports increases so does the likelihood it will belong to the high autonomy category. This is in agreement with the results obtained in the correlation analysis which were opposed to the original hypothesis. The last factor, number of countries in which the parent company has manufacturing subsidiaries, has a negative coefficient (-0.3903). This shows that as the number of countries in which the parent company has manufacturing subsidiares increases so does the likelihood its U.S. subsidiary will enjoy high autonomy for pricing decisions. This result is again in agreement with what we found in the correlation analysis although it is in contradiction with the original hypothesis.

In conclusion we would say that both discriminant analyses give better classifications than obtainable by chance. Not all the variables which are the best discriminators in the multigroup case are the ones found best discriminators in the two group analysis. This result however should not surprise us, since the first case, the objective of the analysis is not necessarily to discriminate between low and high autonomy but rather to find the variables which give the highest overall separation between all the group.

B. Distribution Operational Decisions

Multigroup analysis (Table III Appendix E)

Since the discriminant functions have the ability to separate the groups and the Wilks' Lambda is highly significant and the percentage correctly classified is higher than the proportional change criterion. We may conclude that the three variables: "speed of change in market," "percentage of manufacturing in U.S. for intracompany exports," and "size of intracompany imports to U.S. company as compared to local manufacturing" are the variables which in linear combinations are the best predictors of which specific group a firm should belong to.

Two groups analysis (Table IV Appendix E)

This analysis shows which linear combination of variables discriminate the best between low and high autonomy for U.S. subsidiaries in distribution operation decisions, and how these variables affect the level of autonomy. As can be seen from the groups centroids in reduced space figure, the higher the firm's score for the discriminant function the higher the likelihood it will belong to the high autonomy group (group I).

The factor contributing the most to the discriminant function is the size of intracompany imports to U.S. as compared to local manufacturing (-0.60593). The negative sign of the coefficient shows that the higher the firm's size of intracompany imports to U.S., the higher the likelihood this firm will belong to the low autonomy category.

The second contributing factor is the percentage of manufacturing U.S. for intracompany exports (0.55169). The positive sign of the coefficient shows that the higher a firm's percentage of manufacturing in the U.S. for intracompany exports the higher its likelihood to belong to the high autonomy group.

The next contributing factor is the number of countries in which the parent company has manufacturing subsidiaries (0.46974). The positive sign of the coefficient shows that the larger the number of countries in which the parent company has manufaturing subsidiaries, the higher the likelihood its U.S. subsidiary will belong to the high autonomy category.

Subsidiary performance, the next contributing factor in importance has a negative coefficient (-0.48743) which shows that as the subsidiary's performance improves so does the likelihood it will belong to the low autonomy group.

Finally the last factor, age of subsidiary, has a negative coefficient (-0.34016) which shows that as postulated (as the age of the subsidiary increases) so does its likelihood to belong to the high autonomy category.

We will note that these results are in accordance with our hypotheses except for the percentage of manufacturing U.S. for intracompany exports where the result is in accord with that found in the correlation analysis.

In general we would say that the function discriminates significantly (significant level of Wilks' Lambda and higher percentage of cases correctly classified than if the observation had been classified by chance). The variables affect the level of autonomy either in the way which was expected or in accordance with the correlation results.

C. Advertising and Sales Promotion Operational Decisions

Multigroup analysis (Table V Appendix E)

Here again the discriminant function separates significantly between the groups. While we cannot tell whether a variable has a positive or negative effect on the subsidiary's autonomy in advertising and sales promotion operational decisions, we can however conclude that the factors "technological sophistication of products manufactured," "sensitivity of products of cultural or environmental differences," "width of range of products provided by subsidiary," and "speed of change in market" are in linear combinations good predictors of which control level category a firm should belong to.

Two groups analysis (Table VI Appendix E)

This function shows which linear combination of factors discriminates the best between subsidiaries of low and high autonomy with respect to advertising and sales promotion decisions. The group centroids figure shows that as a firm scores higher on the discriminant function, its likelihood to belong to the high autonomy category is also higher.

The first contributing factor, technological sophistication of products manufactures, has a positive coefficient (0.56303). This shows that as the technology of a firm's products becomes more sophisticated the likelihood this firm will belong to the high autonomy group for advertising and sales promotion decisions increases too. This result is opposite to what was expected, since it was postulated that firms manufacturing technologically sophisticated products would tend to exert more control over their subsidiaries. We have then to conclude that what might be true for certain types of business decisions is not necessarily true for advertising and sales promotions, and that in this particular type of decision, the home-office of subsidiaries manufacturing technologically sophisticated products leave them a lot of autonomy.

The second most important contributing factor is the size of intracompany imports to U.S. as compared to local manufacturing (-0.5413). Again the negative sign shows that as the size of intracompany imports to the U.S. increases, the level of autonomy of the subsidiary for this type of marketing decision tends to decrease.

The third factor is the sensitivity of products to cultural or environmental differences (-0.43496), recalling that as the value of this variable rises, it means that the sensitivity of the firm's products to cultural or environmental differences increases, we can see, that as the sensitivity of a firm's products increases so does the likelihood it will belong to the high autonomy category.

Finally the negative sign of the last factor subsidiary performance (-0.30058) shows that, as postulated, the level of autonomy of a subsidiary tends to increase when its level of performance is good.

In general we might conclude that the discriminant function separates the two autonomy groups significantly (significant level of the Wilks' Lambda and higher percentage of cases correctly classified than if the observations had been classified by chance). Except for "technological sophistication of the products" the variables affect the level of autonomy in advertising and sales promotion operational decisions in the way postulated.

D. New Products Decisions

Multigroups analysis (Table VII Appendix E)

The discriminant functions have a high power of separating the difference autonomy groups for new products decisions (the percentage of cases correctly classified is more than twice as high as the proportional chance criterion).

We can therefore conclude that the variables: "technological sophistication of product," "sensitivity of products to cultural or environmental differences," "size of total corporation," "relative importance of parent company international operation," "width of range of products provided by the subsidiary," "subsidiary performance," "percentage of manufacturing in U.S. for intracompany exports," size of intracompany imports U.S. as compared to local manufacturing," "percentage of ownership by European parent" and "number of countries in which parent company has manufacturing subsidiaries" are good predictors in their linear combination of which autonomy level a firm is likely to belong to for new product decisions.

Two groups analysis (Table VIII Appendix E)

This analysis shows which linear combination of variables discriminate the best between low and high autonomy of the U.S. subsidiaries in new product decisions, and how these variables affect the level of autonomy of the U.S. subsidiaries of European companies for this class of decision.

As can be seen from the group centroids figure, the higher the score of a firm in the discriminant function the higher will be its likelihood of belonging to group 1 (high autonomy).

The factor contributing the most to the discriminant function is the sensitivity of products to cultural or environmental differences (-0.5540) its sign shows that the more sensitive a firm's products are to cultural or environmental differences the higher its likelihood to belong to the high autonomy group.

The second variable is the percentage of ownership by the European parent with a coefficient of -0.47174. This shows again that as the percentage of ownership by the European parent company increases, so does the likelihood its U.S. subsidiary will belong to the low autonomy group in the new products decisions.

Width of the range of products provided by the subsidiary has a coefficient of 0.44033 its positive sign shows that (as postulated) when the width of the range of products provided by the subsidiary increases so does the likelihood it will belong to the high autonomy group.

The fourth factor is subsidiary performance (-0.28260). Its negative sign shows again that firms with low levels of performance will tend to belong to the low autonomy category.

Finally we find again that the size of intracompany imports to U.S. as compared to local manufacturing, has a negative coefficient -0.24839 which shows that as the subsidiary's size of intracompany imports to the U.S. increases, so does the likelihood it will belong to the low autonomy category. This discriminant function separates them significantly between the two groups and the variables have an effect on the subsidiary's autonomy in the way postulated.

E. Physical Characteristics of Products

Multigroup analysis (Table IX Appendix E)

The variables "sensitivity of products to cultural or environmental differences," "U.S. subsidiary relative size" "width of range of products provided by subsidiary," "age of subsidiary," and "speed of change in market" are in linear combination good predictors of which autonomy group a subsidiary is likely to belong to for physical characteristics of the product decisions. This is due to the fact that the Wilks' Lambda is highly significant and the percentage of cases correctly classified much higher than the proportional chance criterion Cpro.

Two groups analysis (Table X Appendix E)

The discriminant function shows that two factors in a linear combination can separate between the two groups of autonomy level for U.S. subsidiaries in physical characteristics of products decisions. We can see from the centroids of group's figure that the higher a firm scores on this function, the higher its likelihood to belong to the low autonomy group.

The first factor, sensitivity of products to cultural or environmental differences, has a coefficient of 0.85139. This positive coefficient shows again that as the sensitivity of a firm's products to cultural or environmental differences increases, so does its likelihood to belong to the high autonomy group.

The second factor is percentage of ownership by the European parent (0.53438); its positive sign shows that as percentage of ownership by European parent increases, so does the likelihood the subsidiary will belong to the low group.

These results are in conformity with what was postulated; we can also see that, since the percentage of cases correctly classified is higher than the proportional chance criterion, the discriminant function separates significantly between the two groups.

F. Brand Name Decisions

Multigroup analysis (Table XI Appendix E)

Discriminant functions have a high power of separating the different autonomy groups for brand name decisions. The percentage of cases correctly classified is much higher than the proportional chance criterion.

The selected variables: "sensitivity of products to cultural or environmental differences," "relative importance of parent company's international operations," "width of range of products provided by the subsidiary," "speed of change in market," "subsidiary performance," "size of intracompany imports to U.S. as compared to local manufacturing," "percentage of ownership," and "number of countries in which parent company has manufacturing subsidiaries" are in linear combinations good predictors of which autonomy category a firm should belong to for brand name decisions.

Two groups analysis (Table XII Appendix E)

This discriminant function has a significant power of separating between low and high autonomy groups (again the percentage of cases correctly classified is higher than the proportional chance criterion). From the centroids of groups in reduced space figure, we can conclude that as a firm gets a higher score on the discriminant function, its likelihood belong to the low autonomy category increases.

The first contributing factor is the sensitivity of products to cultural or environmental differences (0.62646) its positive sign shows that as the sensitivity of a firm's products to cultural or environmental differences increases so does the likelihood it will belong to the high autonomy group.

The second contributing factor is the percentage of ownership by the European parent (0.62154) its positive sign shows that for brand name decisions, the likelihood for a subsidiary to belong to the low autonomy category increases when the percentage of ownership by the European parent increases.

Finally age of subsidiary has a coefficient of -0.40714. This shows that as the age of the subsidiary increases so does the likelihood it will belong to the high autonomy category.

These results are in accordance with our original hypotheses.

G. Packaging and Label Decisions

Multigroup analysis (Table XIII Appendix E)

We find here again that the discriminant function derived from the analysis separate significantly between the groups of different autonomy levels. The variables selected are "sensitivity of products to cultural or environmental differences," "relative importance of the parent company's international operations," "U.S. subsidiary relative size," "width of range of products provided by subsidiary," "speed of change in market," "subsidiary performance," "percentage of manufacturing in U.S. for intracompany exports," "percentage of ownership" and "number of countries in which parent company/ has manufacturing subsidiaries." Their linear combination are good predictors of which autonomy group a subsidiary should belong to for packaging and label decisions.

Two groups analysis (Table XIV Appendix E)

This analysis shows which combinations of factors can separate the firms between those enjoying a high degree of autonomy for their packaging and label decision and those which do not.

The centroids of groups in reduced space figure shows that the higher the score of a firm on the discriminant function the higher the probability this firm will belong to the low autonomy group (category 2).

The highest contributing factor is again sensitivity of products to cultural or environmental differences (0.70987) and its positive sign shows (as for most of the previous decision types) that as the sensitivity of the products of a firm to cultural or environmental differences increases so does its likelihood to belong to the high autonomy group increases.

The negative sign on the coefficient of U.S. subsidiary absolute size (-0.59540) shows that as the absolute size of the U.S. subsidiary increases so does the likelihood it will belong to the high autonomy group.

Finally relative importance of parent company's international operations has a coefficient of 0.52821. The positive sign of this coefficient shows that as the relative importance of the parent company's international operations increases, the level of autonomy of the subsidiary for packaging and label decisions will tend to decrease.

In the overall, this discriminant function separates significantly between the two groups (percentage of cases correctly classified is higher than the proportional chance criterion) and the selected variables affect the level of autonomy for packaging and label decisions the way we hypothesized.

H. Product Line Decisions

Multigroups analysis (Table XV Appendix E)

The discriminant function derived from the analysis separate adequately between the groups since the percentage of cases correctly classified is more than twice as high as the proportional chance criterion. The variables selected as best discriminators between the groups in their linear combination were: "sensitivity of products to cultural or environmental differences," "relative importance of parent company's international operations," "U.S. subsidiary relative size," width of range of products provided by subsidiary," "speed of change in market," "percentage of ownership," and "number of countries in which parent company has manufacturing subsidiaries."

Two groups analysis (Table XVI Appendix E)

This discriminant function shows which linear combination of variables separates between firms enjoying high autonomy for their product lines decisions from those which do not. The ability of the factors to separate between the groups is significant.

From the centroids of groups in reduced space figure we see that the higher the score of a firm on the discriminant function the higher its likelihood to belong to group 1 (high autonomy group). The first contributing variable is width of the range of products provided by the subsidiary (0.72333); its positive coefficient shows that the greater the width of the range of products provided by the subsidiary the higher its likelihood to enjoy a high level of autonomy in product line decisions.

The second contributing variable is sensitivity of products to cultural or environmental differences (-0.59112). The negative coefficent shows that, in the case of product line decisions, the autonomy of a subsidiary will increase with an increase in the sensitivity of its products to cultural or environmental differences. Percentage of ownership by the European parent has a coefficient of -0.43222 which shows that the subsidiary's autonomy for product line decision will be greater when the percentage of ownership by the European parent is lower.

The next factor, technological sophistication of products manufactured has a coefficient of -0.34085. The negative sign of this coefficent shows that for product line decisions the autonomy of the subsidiary will be lower when the technological sophistication of the products manufactured is higher. This result is in an accordance with our original hypothesis although we found for advertising and sales promotion operational decisions that the autonomy of a subsidiary was higher when the technological sophistication of the products it manufactures was higher. We could explain this difference by the fact that it is especially in product-related decisions that the technological sophistication of the products manufactured is a factor of control, since the technically oriented company is generally concerned with maintaining a high level of quality and a constant improvement of products on a worldwide basis. The importance of advertising and sales promotions for these companies might be relatively lower than for less technically oriented firms which have to differentiate their products much more on a promotional and advertising basis in order to compete. These could be the reasons why the parent will exert relatively more control in product related decisions than other firms and less control in advertising and sales promotion decisions than other firms.

Finally, subsidiary performance with a coefficient of -0.29746 shows that as the subsidiary's performance improves the level of control exercised by the parent company in this class of marketing decisions decreases.

All these results are in conformity with the hypotheses which were postulated.

Marketing budgetary decisions

Multigroup analysis (Table XVII Appendix E)

The discriminant functions derived from this analysis separate significantly between the six categories of autonomy in marketing budgetary decisions for U.S. subsidiaries of European companies. The percentage of cases correctly classified is three times the size of the proportional chance criterion.

The variables selected in the stepwise procedure were "sensitivity of products to cultural or environmental differences," "U.S. subsidiary relative size," "width of range of products provided by subsidiary," "subsidiary performance," "percentage of manufacturing in U.S. for intracompany exports," "size of intracompany imports to U.S. as compared to local manufacturing," and "percentage of ownership by the European company."

Two groups analysis (Table XVIII Appendix E)

In this dicriminant function which separates significantly between the firm to be grouped with subsidiaries enjoying a relatively high level of autonomy for marketing budgetary decisions and those belonging to the low autonomy group (group 2), a firm getting a high score will be more likely to belong to the low autonomy group (since the group 2 centroid is higher than the group 1 centroid).

The first factor, percentage of manufacturing U.S. for intracompany exports, has a negative coefficeint (-0.54082) which shows that as the percentage of manufacturing in the U.S. for intracompany export increases the autonomy of the firm for this type of marketing decisions, will be likely to increase too.

Percentage of ownership by the European parent (0.41698) shows that, for this class of decision, the likelihood for a firm to belong to the low autonomy group will be higher if the percentage of ownership by European parents is higher.

The next factor is subsidiary performance (0.40090); it shows that the level of autonomy of a firm will be likely to increase if its performance improves.

Width of the range of products provided by the subsidiary has a coefficient of -0.40015. The negative sign of this coefficient shows that the subsidiary will be more likely to belong to the high autonomy group if the range of products it provides is larger.

The next variable is U.S. subsidiary relative size (-.036022) it shows that the U.S. subsidiary relative size affects positively the level of autonomy in marketing budgetary decisions.

The negative coefficient of age of subsidiary (-0.25609) indicates that as the Age of a subsidiary increases its likelihood to belong to the high autonomy category increases too.

Relative importance of parent company's international operations has a positive coefficient (0.25450) which shows that as the relative importance of the parent company international operation increases so does the likelihood the subsidiary will belong to the autonomy group.

Finally sensitivity of products to cultural or environmental differences has a coefficient of 0.20757; the positive sign of this coefficient shows that as the sensitivity of the firm's products to cultural or enviromental differences increases so does its likelihood to belong to the high autonomy group.

All these results are in conformity with our original hypotheses except for the effect of the percentage of manufaturing in the U.S. for the intracompany exports where the result is in accordance with what was found in the correlation analysis.

Conclusion

The objective of this Chapter has been to check whether and how our postulated variables affect the level of autonomy of U.S. subsidiaries in their marketing decisions. We also wanted to verify whether these variables could predict in which autonomy group a subsidiary would fall for its marketing decisions.

In general, we found that most of our hypotheses were correct. However there were two types of exceptions. The first type concerns those instances when a relation did exist between the postulated factor and the level of autonomy, but the direction of the effect was opposite to that postulated. In the second type of regards those variables which were rarely related to the subsidiary's autonomy in marketing decisions.

Typical of the first type of exceptions, were the variables: "percentage of manufacturing in which the parent company has manufacturing subsidiaries," and "size of the total corporation." For those three variables it was postulated that as their value increased the subsidiary's autonomy should decreaase. In fact the contrary happened and as these variables took higher values the subsidiary autonomy increased.

In the second type of exception we find the variable "technological sophistication of product" for which there was no significant correlation with any of the marketing decision classes. Although it has some discriminating power the direction of its effect on the subsidiary's autonomy in marketing decision is not very clear since in one case it has a negative effect on the subsidiary's autonomy (product line decision) and in another case a positive effect (advertising and sales promotion decisions).

Also two other factors: "U.S. subsidiary relative size," and "relative importance of parent company's international operations" were found significantly correlated to only one type of marketing decision: Pricing decision in the case of "U.S. subsidiary relative size," and "marketing budgetary decision in the case of "relative importance of parent company's international operations."

In fact the variables most often found as main discriminating factors between U.S. subsidiaries enjoying high autonomy for their marketing decision from their European parent and those which do not were: "sensitivity of products to cultural or environmental differences," "subsidiary performance," "percentage of ownership by the European parent," "width of range of products provided by subsidiary," "age of subsidiary," "size of intracompany imports to U.S. as a percentage of local manufacturing," and "percentage of manufacturing in U.S. for intracompany exports." Except for the last factor mentioned, the effect of these variables on subsidiaries' autonomy in marketing decision was always in the direction hypothesized.

The variables which were very often correlated with marketing decision classes were: "sensitivity of products to cultural or environmental differences," "size of total corporation," "U.S. subsidiary absolute size," "width of range of products provided by subsidiary," "speed of change in market," "size of intracompany imports to U.S. as a percentage of local manufacturing," "percentage of ownership," "number of countries in which parent company as manufacturing subsidiaries."

We also found that the difference between the percentage of cases correctly classified and the proportional chance criterion was higher for marketing budgetary decisions and product related decisions than for pricing, advertising and sales promotions and distribution operational decisions. The reason for this is that for marketing budgetary decisions and product related decisions there were many more cases of low autonomy. The proportional chance criterion was therefore much lower than in the other marketing decision classes in which in most cases the subsidiaries enjoyed a considerable amount of autonomy.

In general it can be said that the findings were satisfying: In all decision classes the percentage of cases correctly classified was higher than the proportional chance criterion in the multigroup discriminant analysis and in the two groups discriminant analysis. Most of the hypotheses were confirmed. We can therefore draw the conclusion that the behavior of firms with regard to marketing decisions control is not only a matter of human difference but is also a consequence of some objective factors.

NOTES

[a]Details about the Spearman's r_s coefficient can be found in S. Siegel *Nonparametric Statistics for the Behavioral Sciences.* (McGraw-Hill Book Company, 1965).

[b]The Kendall's correlation coefficients were also measured but since the results were highly similar to the Spearman's r_s coefficients only the Spearman's coefficients are shown.

[c]For more details about the procedure used, see "Statistical Package for the Socal Sciences," Second edi'·on pp. 434-467. (A comprehensive bibliography on the different methods and statistical tests used is given on page 467 of that volume).

[d](This latter measure is based on "the proportional chance criterion" described in Donald G. Morrison's article "On the Interpretation of Discriminant Analysis" *Journal of Marketing Research,* Vol VI, May 1969, pp. 156-163. This proportional chance criterion is equal to Cpro = P (Correct/Classified group I) P (Classified group I) + P (Correct/Classified group II) P (Classified group II) +. . .+P (Correct/Classified group n) P (Classified group n). Where n is the number of groups or categories studies and P means probability. Now, if P_1 is the proportion of cases in group I, P_2 the proportion of cases in group II, pn the proportion of cases in group n, the proportional chance criterion will be equal to Cpro = P_1^2 + P_2^2 +. . .pn^2.

CHAPTER 5

CONCLUSION AND SUGGESTION FOR FURTHER RESEARCH

I. Conclusion

It was found that the the overwhelming majority of U.S. subsidiaries of European companies enjoy a great deal of autonomy in their marketing operational decisions. However, as hypothesized, product policy decisions, physical characteristics of product, brand name, packaging and label, product line involve a greater degree of headquarters control than pricing, distribution, advertising and sales promotion and market research decisions.

The control over marketing budgetary decisions was generally higher than for operational decisions, in accordance with the usual patterns of control behavior in multinational corporations. Even so, a majority of the companies included in this study still enjoyed a great deal of freedom in this type of decision. Previous studies on U.S. companies operating abroad and executive comments indicate that European companies in the U.S. enjoy relatively more autonomy than U.S. subsidiaries in Europe with respect to marketing decisions. However, further research using a methodology similar to that used in this study is needed to investigate objectively the control patterns of U.S. companies over their European subsidiaries. Only this kind of research can lead to truly scientific comparisons.

With regard to the factors affecting the level of autonomy enjoyed by U.S. subsidiaries of European companies for marketing decisions, we tested a certain number of hypotheses by investigating the link between a certain number of pertinent factors (most of them suggested by previous findings and the control level exercised by parent companies on subsidiaries for marketing decisions). The first hypothesis was that the subsidiary's level of autonomy would decrease as the technological sophistication of the products manufactured increased. This hypothesis was not confirmed by the findings.

The next hypothesis was that the level of autonomy of the subsidiary in its marketing decisions would increase as the sensitivity of its products to cultural or enviornmental differences increased. This hypothesis was confirmed by our findings for all marketing decision types.

Another hypothesis was that as the U.S. subsidiary absolute size increased, the level of control exercised by the parent company over marketing decisions would decrease.   This hypothesis was mostly confirmed by the results.   A further hypothesis was that as the size of total corporation (i.e., parent company plus all its subsidiaries and affiliates) increased, the level of control exerted by the parent company over markekting decisions would increase.   The findings show an opposite relation: the level of control decreases for all marketing decision classes as the size of total corporation increases.

One could explain this surprising result by arguing that what is true for American companies operating abroad is not necessarily true for European companies operating in the U.S.   As the total size of the company increases, the European home-office often understaffed at the top will be more likely to delegate powers to the subsidiary's management while for American multinationals an increase in total size is likely to cause head-office management to increase its functional staff and thereby exercise more control over the subsidiaries' activities.

We cannot however exclude the possibility that the original proposition (control increases with size of total corporation) based on the findings of Brooke and Remmers was incorrect and that the inverse relation is in fact the case.   Further research should be conducted in order to assess the true direction of the relation between control of marketing activities and size of total corporation.

It was also hypothesized that control over the subsidiary's marketing decisions by parent companies would increase as the relative importance of the parent company's international operation increased and decrease as the U.S. subsidiary relative size increased.   For the majority of marketing decisions there was insufficient evidence to confirm these hypotheses.

The next hypothesis was that as the width of the range of products provided by the subsidiary increased, the level of autonomy for marketing decisions granted to the subsidiary would increase.   This hypothesis was mostly confirmed by the findings.   There was some supporting evidence that as the age of the subsidiary increased and its performance improved the control over the subsidiary's marketing decision by the parent company would decrease.

The hypothesis that subsidiaries manufacturing product subject to rapid change in the market would be more autonomous was confirmed for most marketing decision types.

It was hypothesized that a large volume of intracompany shipments would generally indicate a certain extent of global interrelated manufacturing.   Since interrelated manufacturing must accommodate the needs of the different companies within the multinational group, it seems logical that the home-office would be more likely to coordinate and monitor the policies of the different subsidiaries.   We therefore expected the subsidiary's level of autonomy for marketing decisions to decrease as the percentage of manufacturing in the U.S. for intracompany exports and/or the size of intracompany imports to the U.S. company increased. If indeed there is some evidence to support the latter hypothesis, the findings suggest an inverse relation for the former: the level of autonomy increases when this percentage of manufacturing for intracompany exports increases.

To explain this paradoxical result, we have to point out first that the correlation between the percentage of manufacturing in the U.S. for intracompany exports and the size of intracompany imports to the U.S. is absolutely insignificant. It would seem therefore that the first premise of our original proposition (i.e., "large volume of intracompany shipments generally indicates a certain extent of interrelated manufacturing") is erroneous since if headquarters had a global policy for interrelated manufacturing it would effect both intracompany exports and imports. In fact the reason why an increase in the percentage of intracompany imports is associated with a decrease in autonomy for most marketing decision areas is that this higher percentage increases the dependence of the subsidiary on the home-office. (We must notify the reader that, in the overwhelming majority of cases, the bulk of these imports came from the parent company and, as this flow of imports increases, the amount of coordination and control by headquarters on most decision areas will also increase.   The subsidiary becomes less and less of a separate entity).

With regard to the increase of the subsidiary's autonomy in relation to the increased percentage of intracompany exports, the plausible explanation is that the intracompany exports of the U.S. subsidiary generally go to subsidiaries not adequately supplied by the home company. In general these subsidiaries are located in the Western hemisphere. Headquarters would consider the U.S. subsidiary a kind of leader in this part of the world, more a regional headquarters than a regular subsidiary. As a consequence the parent company would feel the U.S. company should be granted more autonomy in order to adequately carry out this role.

Our next hypothesis was that as the percentage of ownership by the European parent of the U.S. subsidiary increased, the level of control on marketing decisions would increase. The findings confirm this hypothesis.

Finally, although it was hypothesized that as the number of countries in which the parent company has manufacturing subsidiaries increased, the control exercised over marketing decision would increase, there is evidence to support the contrary phenomenon, reversing the direction of the hypothesized relation.   The explanation for this unexpected result is that, at least for European firms, when the number of countries in which there are operations increases, the home-office - short of adequate managerial staff would rather tend to loosen its control over such activities. Further research should be conducted in order to determine whether American firms behave in a similar way or whether, as they open operations in more and more countries, they create a strong marketing center at headquarters which will coordinate the subsidiaries' activities.

In the last part of this research it was shown that the factors, enumerated above and postulated as affecting the level of control exerted by parent companies over their subsidiaries in marketing decision, had a significant predictive power as to the level of autonomy a subsidiary would enjoy in its marketing decisions. In this last part we also showed for each marketing-decision class which factors were the best indicators for separating the subsidiaries into a low or high autonomy group.

II. Further Research

We have already mentioned that further research may be fruitful in order to test some of the conclusions reached in this study and which may need some more supporting evidence.

The methodology used in this study could be utilized to investigate the way American multinational corporations control the marketing activities of their subsidiaries.   Also, since only U.S. subsidiaries of European companies have been investigated here, it could be of interest to check whether the control level exercised by these companies is similar in the case of non-U.S. subsidiaries.

It might also be fruitful to investigate control of European headquarters over other areas of business than marketing.

Further research might also be conducted in order to assess whether it is more effective for the long run goals of multinational corporations to control closely the marketing activities of subsidiaries or to grant them a large amount of autonomy as is the related issue of checking whether the performance level of a subsidiary can be improved by increasing or decreasing its autonomy level in decision-making.

It might also be of interest to consider whether the amount of autonomy granted to a subsidiary decreases for those decision areas for which the parent company feels it has a competitive distinctiveness and could eventually think that in those areas it should direct its subsidiaries' activities.

Finally, since our study based on data collected in the summer of 1975 is cross-sectional, it would be certainly fruitful to investigate whether the business cycle has any effect on the amount of autonomy granted to a subsidiary. For that purpose it is suggested to follow a number of companies over a period of time in order to assess whether parent companies do exert higher control on their subsidiaries' decisions when as a consequence of a recession profits and sales are lower.

APPENDIX A

Figure I.   Estimate of per capita national income in U.S. Dollars
Statistical Yearbook 1974, United Nations, Table 188

	1960	1963	1970	1971	1972	1973
United States	2559	2856	4289	4980	4984	5554
E.E.C.	1070	1350	1150	2540	2970	. . .
Belgium	1126	1354	2421	2733	3346	. . .
Denmark	1201	1552	2838	3194	3811	5004
France	1202	1570	2550	2831	3403	. . .
W. Germany	1210	1529	2752	3182	3769	5040
Ireland	611	749	1244	1431	1715	2009
Italy	627	896	1531	1735	1984	2298
Luxemburg	1342	1540	2613	2769	3353	4507
Netherlands	880	1092	2232	2587	3165	4103
U.K.	1257	1469	1990	2252	2503	
E.F.T.A.	1030	1290	2230	2520	3010	
Austria	798	991	1730	1987	2453	3350
Finland	1001	1273	1993	2208	2554	3312
Iceland	1178	1526	2047	2573	3163	4313
Norway	1093	1344	2458	2782	3332	4115
Portugal	297	359	684	778	956	
Sweden	1683	2108	3724	4023	4657	5536
Switzerland	1429	1829	2963			

Figure II. Per capita Gross National Product estimates for calendar year 1972 in current market prices U.S. & Compiled by Agency for International Development (See the 1975 *World Almanac and Book of Facts*, Published by Newspaper Enterprise Association for Doubleday, page 587)

Austria	3033
Belgium	4043
Denmark	4557
Finland	3019
France	4213
W. Germany	4693
Iceland	3215
Ireland	1839
Italy	3215
Netherlands	3790
Norway	4071
Sweden	5763
Switzerland	5369
United Kingdom	2714

For calendar year 1972. The U.S. G.N.P. per capita was $5,508.48 according to the U.S. Department of Commerce.

See Almanac above cited pp. 87 and 143.

Figure III. Average annual rate of growth of gross domestic product per capita at constant price - *Statistical Yearbook* 1971 U.N.

Country	Period 1965-70	Period 1960-60
Austria	4.0	3.8
Belgium	3.6	3.9
France	4.9	4.6
Germany	4.0	3.6
Netherlands	4.5	4.0
Sweden	3.2	3.5
Switzerland	3.1	4.0
Italy	5.2	4.4
U.K.	1.7	2.1
United States	2.2	3.2

REMARKS

In 1960 - The G.N.P. per capita in West Germany was 47% of that of the U.S.

In 1973 - According to Figure I it equals 90% of the U.S. G.N.P. per capita.

For Sweden the figures are 66% for 1960 and 101% for Belgium, Denmark, France, West Germany, Norway, Sweden and Switzerland all had by 1972 a G.N.P. per capita at least 75% as big as that of the United States.

From all the countries listed in Figure III only the United Kingdom had a growth rate smaller than the U.S.

APPENDIX B

The distribution of the 56 companies included in the sample according to the nationality of the parent company is as follows:[1]

Nationality of the Parent Company	Number of cases	Percentage
United Kingdom	15	26.8%
France	14	25.0%
Germany	10	17.9%
Switzerland	6	10.7%
Belgium	2	3.6%
Holland	2	3.6%
Italy	2	3.6%
Sweden	2	3.6%
Austria	1	1.8%
Norway	1	1.8%

[1]One company was a subsidiary of a company which was a merger of two companies from two different countries.

With regard to size of the subsidiaries, 15 (or 26.8%) companies included in our sample had an annual sales volume inferior to 10 million dollars in 1974, 25 (or 44.6%) had a sales volume superior to 10 million dollars but inferior to 100 million and 16 (or 28.6%) had a sales volume superior to 100 million dollars.

With regard to the size of the total corporation (including parent company and all the subsidiaries all over the world), 16 or 28.6% of the companies included in our sample belonged to corporations with an annual sales volume in 1974 inferior to 100 million dollars. In 17 or 30.4% of the cases, the annual sales volume of the total corporation was superior to 100 million dollars but inferior to 1 billion and in 22 cases it was superior to 1 billion dollars.

APPENDIX

Breakdown of the sample by Industry

	Number of companies		Percentage
Foods	7		12.5%
Textile mill products	4		7.1%
Apparel and other textile products	3		5.6%
Non electrical machinery	6		10.7%
Electrical and electronic equipment	7		12.5%
Instruments and related products	5		8.9%
Primary metal	2		3.6%
Chemicals	19		33.9%
Flavor and fragrances		4	
Cosmetics, toiletries and perfumes		4	
General and pharmaceuticals		11	
Miscellaneous	3		5.6%

$$\overline{56}$$

APPENDIX C

<u>Questionnaire</u>[1]

- The questionnaire serves both this study and other research projects conducted simultaneously.

- Not all questions asked of the executives of the companies involved with this study show up in this Appendix. For further details see Chapter 2: Methodology.

- Not all the questions were consistently asked in this specific wording to all respondents.

1. To begin our interview, I would like to learn a little about your own background with the company. Could you tell me, please, how long have you been with . . . .?
    (company name)

2. How long have you been in your present position?

3. Before your present position, what other jobs did you hold in the last five years? (Identify which jobs were with the present company).

4. Now would you, please, tell me something about the history of your company in the United States. Specifically I want to know when it was founded? Were products manufactured here in the U.S. from the beginning, or was it initially a sales agency or distributorship? In this latter case, when did the company start to manfacture here?

5. Did your parent company acquire an existing U.S. company or did it establish your subsidiary from scratch? Did it undertake a joint venture?

6. Is your company now totally owned by the parent company? (If no) Approximately what percentage is owned by the parent either directly or indirectly?

7. Is your company here in the U.S. a public company?

8. Is your parent company a public company?

9. a) What are the major products or product groups of your
        company and for what approximate percentage of total
        company sales does each of them account?

    b) Which ones go to the consumer market and which ones to the
        industrial market?

10. a) Now, I would like to know why the parent company decided
        to invest in manufacturing facilities in the U.S. originally?

    b) (Probe): Was it to counter the threats to the market (like
        tariff barriers, competition, antitrust laws. . .)

        to make wider use of its technical lead to achieve geographical
        diversification to learn more sophisticated promotion,
        marketing or product development techniques

    c) Was not a Sales Agency good enough to achieve the parent
        company's goals in the U.S.?

11. a) Is your production solely for the U.S. Market?

    (If no)

    b) Approximately what proportion of sales go to exports,
        including shipment to parent or sister companies?

        (If greater than 5%) Where are the primary markets for those
        exported goods?

    c) What is the proportion of those exports which are intra-
        company shipments?

12. a) Does your parent company have other manufacturing
        subsidiaries in the U.S.?

    (If yes)

    b) Are they all controlled by one office in the U.S.?

    c) Are they manufacturing different products than you do?

13. Does your parent company have manufacturing subsidiaries in
    other countries than in the U.S.?

    (If yes)

Could you tell me where, or if there are too many, in how many countries does your parent company have manufacturing subsidiaries (including the home country)?

14. In how many countries does your parent company have sales and manufacturing subsidiaries?

15. How does the home-office evaluate the performance of your company (Probe) Sales, growth, R.O.I., profit after taxes, ROS, market share. . .

16. How successful is your company compared with other subsidiaries of your parent company?   Well above average, above average, average, below average, considerably below average?

On what basis was this judgment made?

17. Do subsidiaries of your parent company outside the U.S. and/or your parent company itself export into the U.S. market? (If yes)

-   What is the proportion of those exports relative to your production?

-   (In case the parent company has other subsdiaries in the U.S.) What is the proportion of those exports relative to the total U.S. subsidiaries' production?

-   Are those exported products different from those produced here?

-   Which products are exported and which ones are manufactured here?

-   Who is in charge of the exported products in the U.S.?

18. How successful is your company relative to others in your industry in the U.S.? Well above average, above average, average, below average, considerably below average?

19. Is your parent company very satisfied, quite satisfied, somewhat satisfied, not so satisfied or not satisfied at all with the results of your company here in the U.S.

20. a) Could you tell me what were approximately your parent company's total corporate worldwide sales last year?

b)   What percentage of those sales came from outside western Europe?

c)   What percentage of those sales came from outside "country of orgin?"

21.   Could you tell me what were approximately the last year's annual sales of your company in the U.S.?   What proportion of those sales came from local production?

22.   Now let us talk about your products more specifically; what is the average product life cycle of your products?

23.   How much are your products subject to rapid style changes? Very much, quite a lot, somewhat, slightly, not at all?

24.   Do you need a heavy flow of new products in order to compete? Very heavy, quite heavy, somewhat heavy, slightly, not at all?

25.   a)   Do you do research and development in the U.S.?

(If yes)

b)   Do you do basic research?

c)   What is the amount your company in the U.S. spends on research and development in terms of sales percentages?   (If no to (a))

d)   Do you think you need to do some research and development in the U.S.?

26.   What is the amount your parent company spends on research and development in terms of sales percentage?

27.   Are much R and D and engineering inputs needed to develop your products? Very much, quite a lot, some, slight, none at all?

28.   Is it very difficult to design the manufacturing process? Very, quite difficult, somewhat, slightly, not at all?

29.   Is it very difficult to design the product? Very, quite difficult, somewhat, slightly, not at all?

30.   Are there products manufactured by the parent company and not manufactured by you?

(If yes)

Which ones and why?

31.   Are there products which are manufactured by you and not by the parent company?

(If yes)

Which ones and why?

32.   Would you say that you are generally pursuing a diversification or penetration strategy?

33.   What do you consider as your competitive advantage allowing you to compete in the U.S. market?

34.   In many cases a multinational firm has to introduce change in the specification and characteristics of its products in order to adopt them to a foreign environment and/or culture. Would you say that it is the case for your products?   (If yes)

Do you think your products are extremly, very, somewhat, slightly sensitive to environmental and/or cultural difference?

Could you specify what are those differences?

35.   a)   Do you introduce new products in the American market before your parent company does in Europe? Always, often, sometimes, very few times, never?

(If positive)

b)   Why?

c)   Are those products developed here?

36.   Does your parent company consider its operations in the U.S. as a kind of frontier operation, in terms of product or marketing techniques development, which will allow it to make use of the experience gained in the U.S. for other markets? Very much the case, quite a lot, somewhat, not very much, not at all the case?

37. Is your company considered a separate profit center from the parent company?

38. a) Do you need to modify your products, in comparison with the parent company products in order to adapt them to the American market?

(If yes)

b) Does the product need a lot, quite a bit, some or minor modifications?

39. Do you have a marketing department in the U.S.?

40. Do you have a working Board of Directors for your company in the U.S.?

What proportion of the members of the Board of Directors are American residents?

41. Are you financially self-sufficient?

42. During the past two years, which decisions have been most important for the success of your company: Financial decisions, marketing decisions or production decisions? Which have been the second most importnat?

43. I realize that to sell your products, you must integrate many sets of marketing decision but could you tell me which ones among those decisions are critical, very important, important, not so important or not important at all to meet your marketing objectives?

  1. Managing the sales force
  2. Advertising decisions
  3. Sales promotion decisions
  4. Channels of distribution decisions
  5. Finding new markets for the product
  6. Market research
  7. Pricing decisions
  8. Services
  9. Developing and modifying products
  10. Others

44.   Could you tell me how the home-office keeps control of marketing decisions?

45.   a)   Do you have a formal marketing plan?

(If yes)

b)   It is standardized worldwide?

c)   Does your home-office have to approve your marketing plan?

46.   On the overall, could you describe what kind of help, guidance or interference you get from your home-office in these decision areas, and how would you compare with the control exerted by headquarters on marketing decision:

1.   Financial decisions (e.g., leverage, borrowing. . .)?
2.   Personnel?
3.   Research and Development?
4.   Manufacturing?
5.   Purchasing?
6.   Import-export activities?

47.   a)   In general are you satisfied with the level of autonomy you enjoy for those decisions in general and marketing decision in particular?

(If not totally satisfied)

b)   How would you like things to be?

48.   Could you tell me what motivates your parent company to leave you this specific level of autonomy rather than more or less?

49.   a)   Are the above policies, in terms of control exercised over your activities by the parent company, the same for all subsidiaries?

(If the answer is no)

b)   Why are those policies different?

50.   What kind of integrative devices are used by the home-office in order to influence the activities of the worldwide units of the company groups toward a common business pattern?

51. Do you receive any guidelines or manuals of guidance from the home-office in Europe?

52. Do you feel the amount of freedom for your company in the U.S. has increased, decreased or remain the same in the past five years with respect to all decision areas in general and marketing decisions in particular?

53. How do you see the trend for the future?

54. Could you tell me what are approximately your advertising expenditures in terms of percentage of sales?

55. What is the maximum limit you may spend for capital expenditure without prior approval from headquarters?

56. What is the maximum credit you may give to a customer without prior approval from your home-office?

57. What is the maximum amount of money you can spend on advertising without prior approval from the home-office?

58. (Only if the respondent is not the chief executive officer of the company) How long has the chief executive officer of your company been in his function?

NOTES

[1] This questionnaire includes a number of questions that were used by Rocour in his study (6) and by William K. Brandt and James M. Hulbert in their study "Managing the Multinational Subsidiary in Brazil" (see *A Preliminary Summary to Participating Managers*, Research Paper No. 65, July 1974, Graduate School of Business, Columbia University, Uris Hall, New York, N.Y.)

APPENDIX D

SPEARMAN'S CORRELATION COEFFICIENT BETWEEN HYPOTHESIZED FACTORS AND CONTROL OVER MARKETING DECISION CLASSES

Factor \ Marketing Decision Class	Technological Sophistication of Products Manufactured	Sensitivity of Products to Cultural or Environmental Differences	Size of Total Corporation	U.S. Subsidiary Absolute Size
Pricing		Correlation 0.3120 Sig. level 0.012	Correlation -0.2836 Sig. level 0.021	Correlation -0.2141 Sig. level 0.062
Distribution Operational Decisions		Correlation 0.1783 Sig. level 0.099	Correlation -0.1630 Sig. level 0.119	Correlation -0.1508 Sig. level 0.136
Advertising and Sales Promotion Operational Decisions		Correlation 0.3280 Sig. level 0.008	Correlation -0.1813 Sig. level 0.037	
New Products Decisions		Correlation 0.4509 Sig. level 0.001	Correlation -0.2756 Sig. level 0.026	Correlation -0.3364 Sig. level 0.008

Factor / Marketing Decision Class	Relative importance of Parent Company's International Operation	U.S. Subsidiary Relative Size	Width of Range of Products Provided by Subsidary	Age of Subsidiary	Speed of Change in Market
Pricing	Correlation 0.2374 Sig. level 0.060		Correlation -0.2164 Sig. level .060	Correlation -0.2245 Sig. level 0.053	Correlation 0.3031 Sig. level 0.014
Distribution Operational Decisions					
Advertising and Sales Promotion Operational Decisions					Correlation 0.1958 Sig. level 0.078
New Products Decisions			Correlation -0.2998 Sig. level 0.017		

Factor / Marketing Decisions Class	Subsidiary Performance	Percentage of Manufacturing in United States for Intracompany Exports	Size of Intracompany Imports to U.S. as a percentage of local manufacturing	Percentage of Ownership	Numbers of countries in which Parent Company has Manufacturing subsidiaries
Pricing			Correlation 0.1552 Sig. level 0.134	Correlation 0.1710 Sig. level 0.110	Correlation -0.2888 Sig. level 0.023
Distribution Operational Decisions		Correlation -0.3084 Sig. level 0.011	Correlation 0.2957 Sig. level 0.014	Correlation 0.1451 Sig. level 0.145	Correlation -0.2438 Sig. level 0.044
Advertising and Sales Promotion Operational Decisions	Correlation -0.1719 Sig. level 0.110				
New Products Decisions	Correlation -0.2171 Sig. level 0.065		Correlation 0.2903 Sig. level 0.019	Correlation 0.2952 Sig. level 0.018	Correlation -0.3903 Sig. level 0.004

Factor Marketing Decision Class	Technological Sophistication of Products Manufactured	Sensitivity of Products to Cultural or Environmental Differences	Size of Total Corporation	U.S. Subsidiary Absolute Size
Physical Characteristics of the Products		Correlation 0.4780 Sig. level 0.001	Correlation -0.2326 Sig. level 0.052	Correlation -0.1827 Sig. level 0.102
Brand Name Decision		Correlation 0.4885 Sig. level 0.001	Correlation -0.2609 Sig. level 0.065	Correlation -0.3241 Sig. level 0.034
Packaging and Label Decisions		Correlation 0.4024 Sig. level 0.004	Correlation -0.2591 Sig. level 0.065	Correlation -0.2021 Sig. level 0.034
Product Line Decisions		Correlation 0.4013 Sig. level 0.002	Correlation -0.2900 Sig. level 0.019	Correlation -0.3571 Sig. level 0.004
Marketing and Budgetary Decisions		Correlation 0.1568 Sig. level 0.126	Correlation -0.1728 Sig. level 0.104	Correlation -0.2789 Sig. level 0.019

Factor / Marketing Decision Class	Relative importance of Parent Company's International Operation	U.S. Subsidiary Relative Size	Width of Range of Products Provided by Subsidiary	Age of Subsidiary	Speed of Change in Market
Physical Characteristics of the Products			Correlation 0.1804 Sig. level 0.107		Correlation 0.2009 Sig. level 0.081
Brand Name Decision			Correlation -0.2984 Sig. level 0.027	Correlation -0.1912 Sig. level 0.110	Correlation 0.2295 Sig. level 0.069
Packaging and Label Decisions			Correlation -0.2522 Sig. level 0.051		Correlation 0.2253 Sig. level 0.071
Product Line Decisions			Correlation -0.3070 Sig. level 0.013		Correlation 0.1623 Sig. level 0.123
Marketing Budgetary Decisions		Correlation -0.1841 Sig. level 0.89		Correlation -0.1784 Sig. level 0.94	

Factor / Marketing Decision Class	Subsidiary Performance	Percentage of Manufacturing in United States for Intracompany Exports	Size of Intracompany Imports to U.S. as a percentage of local manufacturing	Percentage of Ownership	Numbers of countries in which Parent Company has Manufacturing Subsidiaries
Physical Characteristics of the Products		Correlation -0.1622 Sig. level 0.130		Correlation 0.1741 Sig. level 0.113	
Brand Name Decision	Correlation -0.2578 Sig. level 0.050			Correlation 0.3075 Sig. level 0.022	Correlation -0.3053 Sig. level 0.031
Packaging and Label Decisions		Correlation -02272 Sig. level 0.069		Correlation 0.2190 Sig. level 0.077	Correlation -0.2093 Sig. level 0.097
Product Line Decisions			Correlation 0.2903 Sig. level 0.019	Correlation 0.3137 Sig. level 0.011	Correlation -0.3255 Sig. level 0.012
Marketing Budgetary Decisions		Correlation -0.3055 Sig. level 0.011	Correlation 0.2605 Sig. level 0.026	Correlation 0.4171 Sig. level 0.001	Correlation -0.1796 Sig. level 0.104

APPENDIX E

TABLE I

PRICING DECISIONS

Multigroup Analysis

DISCRIMINANT	EIGENVALUE	RELATIVE PERCENTAGE
1	0.43374	67.81
2	0.19265	30.12
3	0.01327	2.07

STANDARDIZED DISCRIMINANT FUNCTION COEFFICIENTS

	FUNC 1	FUNC 2	FUNC 3
Technological sophistication of products manufactured.	-0.58066	-0.29442	0.12846
Sensitivity of products to cultural or environmental differences.	-0.56391	0.31725	0.03870
Relative importance of parent company's international operations.	-0.23423	0.48819	-0.53272
Width of the range of products provided by the subsidiary.	0.82408	0.10464	-0.48213
Subsidary performance.	-0.37189	-0.64238	-0.60952
Percentage of manufacturing U.S. for intracompany exports.	0.07380	0.63302	-0.31864

Wilks' Lambda = 0.57715 its significance level is 0.105

The percentage of cases correctly classified is 88.68% while the proportional chance criterion Cpro is $(.811)^2 + (.113)^2 + (.038)^2 + (.038)^2 = 0.673$ or 67.3%

TABLE II

PRICING DECISIONS

Two Groups Analysis

STANDARDIZED DISCRIMINANT FUNCTION COEFFICIENTS

FUNC 1

Speed of change in
market.   0.60030

Subsidiary performance.   0.69907

Percentage of manufac-
turing U.S. for intra-
company exports.   -0.45858

Number of countries in which
the parent company has manufacturing subsidiaries.   -0.39003

CENTROIDS OF GROUPS IN REDUCED SPACE

FUNC 1

GROUP 1   -0.12480

GROUP 2   1.52884

Wilks' Lambda = 0.80553, its significance level is 0.031.

Percentage of cases correctly classified is 94.34% while the proportional chance criterion Cpro is $(.925)^2 + (.075)^2 =$
.8603 or 86.03%.

TABLE III

DISTRIBUTION OPERATIONAL DECISIONS

A) Multigroup Analysis

DISCRIMINANT FUNCTION	EIGENVALUE	RELATIVE PERCENTAGE
1	0.29981	79.49
2	0.06936	18.39
3	0.00801	2.12

STANDARDIZED DISCRIMINANT FUNCTION COEFFICIENTS

	FUNC 1	FUNC 2	FUNC 3
Speed of change in market.	0.18109	0.99498	0.03881
Percentage of manufacturing U.S. for intra-company exports.	-0.44443	0.02603	-0.90055
Size of intracompany imports to U.S. as compared to local manufacturing.	0.89224	-0.01689	-0.46970

Wilks' Lambda = 0.71372. Its significance level is 0.048.

The percentage of cases correctly classified is 90.91% while the proportional chance criterion Cpro is $(.873)^2 + (.018)^2 + (.031)^2 + (.018)^2 = 0.7992$ or 79.92%.

TABLE IV

DISTRIBUTION OPERATIONAL DECISIONS

<u>Two groups analysis</u>

	FUNC 1
Age of subsidiary.	-0.34016
Subsidiary performance.	-0.48743
Percentage of manufactur- ing U.S. for intracompany Exports.	0.55169
Size of intracompany imports to U.S. as compared to local manufacturing.	-0.60593
Number of countries in which the parent company has manufactur- ing subsidiaries.	0.46974

CENTROIDS OF GROUPS IN REDUCED SPACE

	FUNC 1
GROUP 1	0.15961
GROUP 2	-1.30350

Wilks' Lambda is 0.7881.   Its significance level is 0.034.

The percentage of cases correctly classified is 92.73% while the proportional chance criterion Cpro is equal to $(.891)^2 + (.109)^2 = .8055$ or 80.55%.

TABLE V

ADVERTISING AND SALE PROMOTION OPERATIONAL DECISION

Multigroup Analysis

DISCRIMINANT	EIGENVALUE	RELATIVE PERCENTAGE
1	0.63428	82.39
2	0.10693	13.89
3	0.02634	3.42
4	0.00233	0.30

STANDARDIZED DISCRIMINANT FUNCTION COEFFICIENTS

	FUNC 1	FUNC 2	FUNC 3	FUNC 4
Technological sophistication of products manufactured.	0.14859	-1.17459	-0.34772	-0.29329
Sensitivity of products to cultural or environmental differences.	-0.65043	0.01890	-0.79717	-0.05323
Width of the range of products provided by the subsidiary.	0.40809	0.68665	-0.23614	0.96180
Speed of change in market.	0.78035	0.75633	-0.24888	-0.29494

Wilks' Lambda is 0.5375 with a significance level = of 0.017

Percentage of cases correctly classified is 77.78% while the proportional chance criterion Cpro is equal to $(.741)^2 + (.111)^2 + (.093)^2 + (.019)^2 + (.037)^2 = .571$ or 57.1%.

TABLE VI

ADVERTISING AND SALES PROMOTION OPERATIONAL DECISION

Two Groups Analysis

STANDARDIZED DISCRIMINANT FUNCTION COEFFICIENTS

	FUNC 1
Technological sophistication of products manufactured.	0.56303
Sensitivity of products to cultural or environmental differences.	−0.43496
Subsidiary performance.	−0.30058
Size of intracompany imports to U.S. as compared to local manufacturing	−0.54139

CENTROIDS OF GROUPS IN REDUCED SPACE

	FUNC 1
GROUP 1	0.18258
GROUPS 2	−1.04982

Wilks' Lambda is 0.80478 with a significance level of 0.028.

The percentage of cases correctly classified is 88.89% while the proportional chance criterion Cpro is equal to $(.852)^2 +$ $(.148)^2 = .7475$ or 74.75%.

TABLE VII

NEW PRODUCTS DECISIONS

Multigroup Analysis

DISCRIMINANT FUNCTION	EIGENVALUE	RELATIVE PERCENTAGE
1	1.22810	49.77
2	0.64363	26.08
3	0.36614	14.84
4	0.22916	9.31

STANDARDIZED DISCRIMINANT FUNCTION COEFFICIENTS

	FUNC 1	FUNC 2	FUNC 3	FUNC 4
Technological sophistication of products manufactured.	−0.27021	0.07601	−0.76512	−0.23438
Sensitivity of products to cultural or environmental differences.	0.60487	0.59045	−0.39370	−0.10876
Size of total corporation.	−0.52560	0.07885	−0.21240	1.13537
Relative importance of parent company's international operations.	−0.03235	−0.68230	−0.11264	0.08662
Width of the range of products provided by the subsidiary.	0.04267	−0.40757	0.67905	−0.65023
Subsidiary performance.	0.49232	−0.37008	0.01653	−0.43121
Percentage of manufacturing U.S. for intracompany exports.	0.35500	0.10749	0.48734	0.30062
Size of intracompany imports to U.S. as compared to local manufacturing.	0.26628	−0.45947	0.09695	−0.08267

TABLE VII (con't.)

	FUNC 1	FUNC 2	FUNC 3	FUNC 4
Percentage of ownership by the European parent.	-0.02736	-0.0653-	-0.41003	0.61700
Number of countries in which the parent company has manufacturing subsidiaries.	0.22772	0.51210	0.14204	-0.65886

Wilks' Lambda is 0.16255 with a significance level of 0.001.

Percentage of cases correctly classified as 72.55% while the proportional chance Criterion Cpro is $(.51)^2 + (.078)^2 + (.216)^2 + (.137)^2 + (.059)^2 = .3346$ or 33.46%.

TABLE VIII

NEW PRODUCTS DECISIONS

Two Groups Analysis

STANDARDIZED DISCRIMINANT FUNCTION COEFFICIENTS

FUNC 1

	FUNC 1
Sensitivity of products to cultural or environmental differences.	-0.55400
Width of the range of products provided by the subsidiary.	0.44033
Subsidiary performance.	-0.28260
Size of intracompany imports to U.S. as compared to local manufacturing.	-0.24839
Percentage of ownership by the European parent.	-0.47174

CENTROIDS OF GROUPS IN REDUCED SPACE

	FUNC 1
GROUP 1	0.46737
GROUP 2	-0.66768

Wilks' Lambda is 0.68170 its significance level is 0.004

Percentage of cases correctly classified is 72.55% while the proportional chance criterion Cpro is $(.588)^2 + (.412)^2$ = .5165 = 51.56%

TABLE IX

PHYSICAL CHARACTERISTICS OF THE PRODUCTS

Multigroup Analysis

DISCRIMINANT FUNCTION	EIGENVALUE	RELATIVE PERCENTAGE
1	0.76632	53.86
2	0.39110	27.49
3	0.20902	14.69
4	0.05648	3.97

STANDARDIZED DISCRIMINANT FUNCTION COEFFICIENTS

	FUNC 1	FUNC 2	FUNC 3	FUNC 4
Sinsitivity of products to cultural or environmental differences.	0.61965	0.32313	0.80203	-0.29656
U.S. subsidiary relative size.	0.43624	-0.21201	-0.04621	-0.14261
Width of the range of products provided by the subsidiary.	-0.39916	-0.19466	-0.28220	-0.37168
Age of subsidiary.	0.05390	0.47432	0.36158	0.83641
Speed of change in market.	0.05037	-0.89036	0.29578	0.34404

The Wilks' Lambda is 0.31862 with a significance level of 0.0001

The percentage of cases correctly classified is 66% while the proportional chance criterion Cpro is $(.58)^2 + (.16)^2 + (.08)^2 + (.12)^2 + (.06)^2 = .3864$ or 38.64%

TABLE X

PHYSICAL CHARACTERISTICS OF THE PRODUCTS

Two Groups Analysis

STANDARDIZED DISCRIMINANT FUNCTION COEFFICIENTS

FUNC 1

Sensitivity of products
to cultural or environ-
mental differences.   0.85139

Percentage of ownership
by the European parent.   0.53438

CENTROIDS OF GROUPS IN REDUCED SPACE

FUNC 1

GROUP 1   -0.25562

GROUP 2   0.72753

Wilks' Lambda is .81021 its significance level is 0.009

The percentage of cases correctly classified is 76% while
the proportional chance criterion Cpro is $(.74)^2 + (.26)^2 = .6152$

TABLE XI

BRAND NAME DECISIONS

Multigroup Analysis

DISCRIMINANT FUNCTION	EIGENVALUE	RELATIVE PERCENTAGE
1	1.19006	59.26
2	0.55736	27.75
3	0.23657	11.78
4	0.02425	1.21

STANDARDIZED DISCRIMINANT FUNCTION COEFFICIENTS

	FUNC 1	FUNC 2	FUNC 3	FUNC 4
Sensitivity of products to cultural or environmental differences.	-0.83199	0.23499	0.01763	-0.11691
Relative importance of parent company's international operations.	0.08899	-0.40662	0.75198	0.18565
Width of the range of products provided by the subsidiary.	0.61766	-0.17745	-0.35659	0.22396
Speed of change in market.	0.00181	-0.24918	-0.90037	-0.39867
Subsidiary performance.	0.11145	-0.1145	-0.72629	0.21248
Size of intracompany imports to U.S. as compared to local manufacturing.	0.23610	-0.23610	-0.38660	-0.73485
Percentage of ownership by the European parent.	-0.42550	0.05575	-0.11263	0.58865
Number of countries in which the parent company has manufacturing subsidiaries.	-0.26887	0.64309	-0.43545	-0.19774

Table XI (con't)

Wilks' Lambda is 0.23149;   its significance level is 0.015

The percentage of cases correctly classified is 69.77%
while the proportional chance criterion is $(.512)^2$ +
$(.07)^2 + (.186)^2 + (.116)^2 + (.116)^2$ = .3281 or 32.81%

TABLE XII

BRAND NAME DECISIONS

Two Groups Analysis

STANDARDIZED DISCRIMINANT FUNCTION COEFFICIENTS

FUNC 1

Sensitivity of products
to cultural or environ-
mental differences.   0.62646

Age of subsidiary.   -0.40714

Percentage of ownership
by the European parent.   0.62154

CENTROIDS OF GROUPS IN REDUCED SPACE

FUNC 1

GROUP I   -0.37359

GROUP 2   0.51887

The Wilks' Lambda is 0.80153 with a significance level of 0.032

The percentage of cases correctly classified is 74.42%
while the proportional chance criterion Cpro is $(.581)^2$
+ $(.419)^2$ = .5132 or 51.32%

TABLE XIII

PACKAGING AND LABEL DECISIONS

Multigroup Analysis

DISCRIMINANT FUNCTION	EIGENVALUE	RELATIVE PERCENTAGE
1	0.96079	41.89
2	0.88308	38.50
3	0.33429	14.57
4	0.11551	5.04

STANDARDIZED DISCRIMINANT FUNCTION COEFFICIENTS

	FUNC 1	FUNC 2	FUNC 3	FUNC 4
Sensitivity of products to cultural or environmental differences.	−0.64303	0.23901	−0.30748	0.27409
Relative importance of parent company's international operations.	−0.84496	−0.49888	0.03452	−0.56975
U.S. subsidiary relative size.	0.25187	0.48479	0.01919	0.58884
Width of the range of products provided by the subsidiary.	0.43297	−0.61222	0.02292	0.61719
Speed of change in market.	0.53102	−0.12931	−0.54678	−0.00410
Subsidiary performance.	0.39579	−0.11455	−0.24256	0.23944
Percentage of manufacturing U.S. for intracompany exports.	−0.29554	−0.15410	0.39701	0.25668

Table XIII (con't)

Percentage of ownership by the European parent.	0.00437	0.39236	-0.39003	0.03052
Number of countries in which the parent company has manufacturing subsidiaries.	0.36196	0.93009	0.17376	0.25571

Wilks' Lambda is 0.18196; its significance level is 0.006.

Percentage of cases correctly classified is 77.27% when
the proportional chance criterion Cpro is $(.568)^2 + (.091)^2$
$+ (.182)^2 + (.068)^2 + (.091)^2 = .3770$ or 37.70%

TABLE XIV

PACKAGING AND LABEL DECISIONS

Two Groups Analysis

STANDARDIZED DISCRIMINANT FUNCTION COEFFICIENTS

FUNC 1

Sensitivity of products to cultural or environmental differences.	0.70987
U.S. subsidiary absolute size.	-0.59540
Relative importance of parent company's international operations.	0.52821

CENTROIDS OF GROUPS IN REDUCED SPACE

RUNC 1

GROUP 1   -0.37444

GROUP 2   0.72391

The Wilks' Lambda is 0.72264; its significance level is 0.005.

The percentage of cases correctly classified is 81.82% while the proportional chance criterion is $(.659)^2 + (3.41)^2 =$

.5509 or 55.09%

TABLE XV

PRODUCT LINE DECISIONS

Multigroup Analysis

DISCRIMINANT FUNCTION	EIGENVALUE	RELATIVE PERCENTAGE
1	0.75542	50.39
2	0.42091	28.08
3	0.30509	20.35
4	0.01764	1.18

STANDARDIZED DISCRIMINANT FUNCTION COEFFIEIENTS

	FUNC 1	FUNC 2	FUNC 3	FUNC 4
Sensitivity of products to cultural or environmental differences.	-0.63851	0.18992	-0.46190	-0.27104
Relative importance of parent company's international operations.	-0.20320	0.34565	0.78383	-0.50440
U.S. subsidiary relative size.	-0.18423	-0.65732	-0.15507	-0.23001
Width of the range of products provided by the subsidiary.	0.53708	-0.21929	0.21226	-0.12393
Speed of change in market	0.58452	0.52135	-0.54793	-0.29417
Percentage of ownership by the European parent.	-0.33374	0.29221	-0.14944	0.48653

Table XV (con't)

| Number of countries in which the parent company has manufacturing subsidiaries. | 0.00847 | −0.49797 | −0.84805 | −0.01534 |

Wilks' Lambda is 0.30186 with a significance level of 0.002.

The percentage of cases correctly classified is 66.04% while the proportional chance criterion Cpro is $(.472)^2 + (.113)^2 + (.264)^2 + (.119)^2 + (.038)^2 = .3124$ or 31.24%

TABLE XVI

PRODUCT LINE DECISIONS

Two Groups Analysis

STANDARDIZED DISCRIMINANT FUNCTION COEFFICIENTS

                                        FUNC 1

Technological sophis-
tication of products
manufactures.   -0.34085

Sensitivity of pro-
ducts to cultural or
environmental differ-
ences.   -0.59112

Width of the range of
products provided by
the subsidiary.   0.72333

Subsidiary performance.   -0.29746

Percentage of owner-
ship by the European
parent.   -0.43222

CENTROIDS OF GROUPS IN REDUCED SPACE

                        FUNC 1

GROUP 1   0.47734

GROUP 2   -0.67262

Wilks' Lambda is 0.67275;   its level of significance os 0.002.

The percentage of cases correctly classified is 73.58%
while the proportional chance criterion Cpro is
$(.585)^2 + (.415)^2 = .5144$ or 51.44%

TABLE XVII

MARKETING BUDGETARY DECISIONS

Multigroup Analysis

DISCRIMINANT FUNCTION	EIGENVALUE	RELATIVE PERCENTAGE
1	1.29826	60.03
2	0.40662	19.26
3	0.30816	14.25
4	0.09779	4.52
5	0.04195	1.94

STANDARDIZED DISCRIMINANT FUNCTION COEFFICIENTS

	FUNC 1	FUNC 2	FUNC 3	FUNC 4	FUNC 5
Sensitivity of products to cultural or environmental differences.	0.38659	-0.22546	-0.48438	0.68775	0.23781
U.S. subsidiary relative size.	-0.48878	0.08942	0.11906	0.03457	-0.05079
Width of the range of products provided by the subsidiary.	-0.14897	-0.53500	-0.50645	-0.00734	-0.49813
Subsidiary performance.	0.13141	0.76532	0.08332	0.33358	-0.32255
Percentage of manufacturing U.S. for intracompany exports.	-0.50666	-0.29671	-0.15660	0.09040	0.39102
Size of intracompany imports to U.S. as compared to local manufacturing.	-0.09781	-0.36676	0.72353	0.46663	-0.09206

Table XVII (con't)

Percantage of
ownership by the
European parent.   0.62042   -0.30750   0.15759   -050453   -0.41240

Wilks' Lambda is 0.20526;   its significance level is 0.0001

Percentage of cases correctly classified is 55.36% while
the proportional chance criterion is $(.268)^2 + (.616)^2 +$
$(.179)^2 + (.071)^2 + (.125)^2 + (.196)^2 = .1885$ or 18.85%

TABLE XVIII

MARKETING BUDGETARY DECISIONS

E) TWO GROUPS ANALYSIS

STANDARDIZED DISCRIMINANT FUNCTION COEFFICIENTS

	FUNC 1
Sensitivity of products to cultural or environmental differences	0.20757
Relative importance of parent company's international operations	0.25450
U.S. subsidiary relative size	-0.36002
Width of the range of products provided by subsidiary	-0.40015
Age of subsidiary	-0.25609
Subsidiary performance	0.40090
Percentage of manufacturing in U.S. for intra-company exports	-0.54082
Percentage of ownership	0.41698

CENTROIDS OF GROUPS IN REDUCED SPACE

	FUNC 1
GROUP 1	-0.54406
GROUP 2	0.84083

Wilks' Lambda is 0.5342; its significance level is 0.0001

The percentage of cases correctly classified is 80.36% while the proportional chance criterion Cpro is $(.607)^2 + (.393)^2$ = .5230 or 52.30%

BIBLIOGRAPHY

ALSEGG R.J. "Control Relationship between American Corporations and their European Subsidiaries," *A.M.A. Research Study* 102.

ARPAN, J.S. and David A. Ricks, "Directory of Foreign Manufacturing in the U.S.," Publishing Service Division School of Business Administration, Georgia State University, Atlanta, Georgia, 1975.

ARPAN, J.S. and David A. Ricks, "Multinational Firms Strategy," Vol. 1, Indiana University Bureau of Business Research, Bloomington, Indiana, 1975.

AYLMER, R.J. "Who Makes Marketing Decisions in the Multinational Firm?" *Journal of Marketing* Vol. 34 (October, 1970), 25-39.

BAKER, J.C. "Multinational Marketing: A comparative Case Study" in Bernard A. Marin "Marketing in a Changing World," Chicago American Marketing Association, 1969, 61-64.

BRITT, S.H. "Standardizing Marketing for the International Market, *"The Columbia Journal of World Business,"* (Winter 1974).

BROOKE, M.Z. and H.L. Remmers, "The Strategy of Multinational Enterprise, Organization and Finance," American Elsevier Publishing Company Inc., New York, 1970, 88.

BUZZEL, R. "Can You Standardize Multinational Marketing?" *Harvard Business Review,* (November, 1968).

Foreign Direct Investors in the United States. List of Foreign Firms with some interest/control in American manufacturing and petroleum companies in the United States: A United States Department of Commerce Publication 1973. See also the "Addendum to the October 1973 list." March 1, 1974.

FRANKO, L.G. "European Business Strategies in the United States," *Business International S.A.,* 1971.

FRANKO, L.G. "Strategy Structure Frustration the Experience of European Firms in America," *European Business,* Autumn 1971, 29-42.

KEEGAN, W.J. "Multinational Marketing: The Headquarters Role," *Columbia Journal of World Business,* Vol. VI, no. 1 (January-February 1961).

KEEGAN, W.J. "Multinational Marketing Control," *Journal of International Business Studies,* Fall 1972.

KEEGAN, W.J. "Multinational Marketing Management," Prentice Hall, 1974, 525-526.

LEFTWICH, R.B. "Foreign Direct Investment in the United States 1962 - 71," *Survey of Current Business,* February 1973.

LEFTWICH, R.B. "Foreign Direct Investment in the U. S. in 1973." *Survey of Current Business,* August 1974, Part II.

ROBINSON, R.D. "International Business Management, A Guide to Decision-Making," Holt, Rinehart and Winston, Inc., 1973, 587.

ROBOCK, S. and K. Simmonds, *International Business and Multinational Enterprises* (Richard D. Irwin, Inc., 1973) 457-459.

ROBOCK, S. "The Silent Invasion."

ROCOUR, J.L. "Management of European Corporate Subsidiaries in the United States." (Unpublished Ph.d. dissertation, Cornell University, September 1973).

ROCOUR, J.L. "Management of European Subsidiaries in the U.S.," *Management International Review* (1966/1).

SKINNER, W. "American Industry in Developing Economics," John Wiley and Sons, Inc., 1968, 191.

STOPFORD, J.M. and L.T. Wells, Jr. "Managing the Multinational Enterprise/Organization of the Firm and Ownership of the Subsidiaries," Basic Book Inc., New York, 1968, 22.

U.S. Department of Commerce Office of Business Economics, *Foreign Business Investments in the United States* by S. Pizer and Z. Warner (Washington D.C. U.S. Government Printing Office 1962) Table IV.

WIECHMAN, U.E. "Integrating Multinational Marketing Activities," *Columbia Journal of World Business,* Winter 1974.

WIND, Y. and Susan P. Douglas, Howard V. Perlmutter, "Guidelines for Developing International Marketing Strategies," *Journal of Marketing,* April 1973.